CHARLES DICKENS
and his world

J. B. PRIESTLEY

CHARLES DICKENS
and his world

CHARLES SCRIBNER'S SONS

NEW YORK

Originally published in the United States by Viking Press, 1969

1 3 5 7 9 11 13 15 17 19 I/C 20 18 16 14 12 10 8 6 4 2

Printed in Great Britain
Library of Congress Catalog Card Number 77–90490
ISBN 0–684–15574–5

Chatham in the early nineteenth century

CHARLES DICKENS WAS BORN IN LANDPORT, now part of Ports-mouth, on February 7, 1812. He was the second child and the eldest son of John and Elizabeth Dickens. John Dickens, whose parents belonged to the higher ranks of domestic service, was a clerk in the Navy Pay Office. He was a lively good-hearted man, fond of convivial evenings and of a pompously ora-torical style of speech, over-optimistic and careless about money and never able to live long within his income. (These traits of course appear in Micawber, just as certain characteristics of Dickens's mother can be found in Mrs Nickleby. It is a mistake, however, to imagine that characters of this kind—and there are many in Dickens—can be regarded as portraits or even as direct caricatures. Dickens created a world of his own, and his characters belong to that world.) Charles's mother was born Elizabeth Barrow, and was the daughter of Charles Barrow, for years a Chief Conductor of Money for the Navy Board. But only a few months after Elizabeth had married John Dickens, it was discovered that Charles Barrow had been falsifying his accounts, robbing the Navy Board of more than five thousand pounds, and he escaped a prison sentence only by leaving England for the Continent.

Elizabeth Dickens (*née* Barrow), Charles's mother

John Dickens, Charles's father

This was the first piece of bad luck for the young Dickens couple, soon to be dogged by misfortune and with six children to support. After a short period in London, John Dickens in 1817 was transferred to the dockyard at Chatham, and here the family remained until 1822. These were the happiest years of Charles Dickens's childhood and youth, and this corner of Kent, with Rochester as its centre, strongly influenced both his life and his work. It was here, years later when he was at the height of his fame, that he returned to live, buying Gad's Hill Place, the very house that he and his father had so often admired when out walking. It was here, after twelve years at Gad's Hill, that he died. And Rochester, the countryside around it, the Thames Estuary not far away, make their appearances, under various names, in book after book.

The little boy, eager, bright, sensitive, energetic but not really robust, found life opening out for him wonderfully during these years at Chatham. He dis-covered books—*Don Quixote*, *Gil Blas*, the comic picaresque novels of Smollett. He discovered the Theatre, to which he was taken at an unusually early age. If his impecunious father was already getting into difficulties, compelling him

The Dickens's house in Chatham

Old Rochester High Street

even then to move into a smaller house, Charles was still too young to understand and to share the strain. This was the golden time, to which the weary
celebrity, buying Gad's Hill Place so many years later, longed to return.

His recollections of these years, seen in the golden haze of childhood, played
a very important part in his work. They help to explain why his earlier novels
are never strictly contemporary but appear to be set back in time, somewhere
around 1820, especially in their happier passages. There is a child's memory at
work in the creation of the Dickens world, in its unique combination of sharply
realistic detail and a fairytale atmosphere. There remained alive in the great
novelist the small boy who walked with his father from Chatham to Rochester,
who stared at the coaches and the old inns. (It is worth remarking here that the
very critics who welcomed a highly subjective method in fiction usually failed
to remember, if they ever knew, that in the childhood chapters of *David Copperfield* Dickens had led the way.) If he had not had this happy time, brightening

The countryside around
Rochester where Dickens
played as a child

A coaching scene of the period

The house in Bayham Street,
Camden Town

his childhood, the novels of Dickens would have been darker and bleaker. On the other hand, because it came so early and was so comparatively brief and was followed by much misery, it left him with a sense of loss—of 'something wanting'—that was to haunt him to the end of his life.

The misery began in 1823, after John Dickens had been recalled to London and had settled in a very small house in Camden Town. He had left Chatham sadly in debt, even after selling off some of his furniture, and nobody in London came to the rescue of John and Elizabeth Dickens and their six children. Everything that could be dispensed with went to the pawnshop, and young Charles was frequently sent on errands of this sort. For he was no longer going to school. He had done well at school in Chatham, where his schoolmaster presented him with a copy of Goldsmith's *Bee* 'as a keepsake'. But his harassed parents had made no plans for him to continue his education in London. His elder sister Fanny had been lucky, winning a pupil-boarder's scholarship at the Royal Academy of Music, but the eleven-year-old Charles, eager to learn and now denied even the few books the family had possessed, was out of all luck. It was as if his father, as Dickens wrote afterwards, had clean forgotten that his son had any claim to be educated: 'So I degenerated into cleaning his boots of a morning, and my own; and making myself useful in the work of the little house; and looking after my younger brothers and sisters (we were now six in all); and going on such poor errands as arose out of our poor way of living.' Living in an atmosphere of debts, decay and threatened disaster, feeling neg- lected and forlorn, and probably not getting enough to eat, the boy was already nervously apprehensive, beginning to suffer in health, when fate dealt him a blow from which, at heart, he never really recovered. The move, as many such things are, was actually well-meant. A friend of the family had an interest in a blacking warehouse, and he suggested that Charles should go to work there, earning six shillings a week. His parents instantly agreed, and there the boy went.

We have been told—by Somerset Maugham among others—that Dickens and his admirers have made too much out of this blacking warehouse episode. The place may have been dark, dirty, rat-infested, but young Charles was not ill-treated or over-worked; it was common enough, at that time and much later, for boys of twelve to go out to work; and he did not in fact remain there very long. But the critics who make light of this episode are not persons who found themselves shut out of school, at the age of twelve, to work in blacking warehouses. They are forgetting what it is like to be a child in utter despair.

The little boy in
the blacking warehouse

Dickens could not forget. 'No words can express the secret agony of my soul,' he wrote, years afterwards, 'as I sunk into this companionship, compared these every day associates with those of my happier childhood; and felt my early hopes of growing up to be a learned and distinguished man, crushed in my breast. . . . My whole nature was so penetrated with the grief and humiliation of such considerations, that even now, famous and caressed and happy, I often forget in my dreams that I have a dear wife and children; even that I am a man; and wander desolately back to that time in my life . . .' The wound was deep and may be said never to have healed. It was not of course the actual business of pasting on blacking labels that did the mischief. It was the feeling of being thrust, uncared for, in a dark blind alley that wounded him so deeply. After the bright years at Chatham, it was like turning a corner and finding himself, without any hope of escape, in a nightmare. Much of the darkness in Dickens, sinister, menacing, murderous, comes from this time.

Only a few days after Charles started work at the blacking warehouse, which was at Hungerford Stairs, his father was arrested and sent to the debtors' prison, the Marshalsea. Later, John Dickens was joined by his wife and the

Old Hungerford Stairs by the Thames

The Marshalsea debtors' prison where John Dickens was sent for debt

younger children. He was still receiving pay from the Navy Board, and though they all had to make do with one room in the Marshalsea, they were probably rather better off in this free lodging than they had been outside, keeping creditors at bay and pawning the spoons. Little Charles came and went, running many errands for his father at the week-end, but he did not live in the prison, a room being found for him nearby. The twelve-year-old boy had to feed himself. Undernourishment, loneliness, misery, brought on several very painful seizures, as we know from Dickens's later account of this time. It came to an end when John Dickens's mother died, leaving him sufficient to pay his debts. Free to leave the Marshalsea, Mrs Dickens found a small house in Somers Town. Charles was still working at the blacking warehouse, though now it had been moved to larger premises, at the corner of Bedford Street, Covent Garden. There the boy sat in one of the windows, pasting on his labels in full view of the street, and John Dickens caught sight of him at work. He made up his mind that his son should leave the blacking warehouse, in spite of the fact that his wife wanted the boy to remain there. 'I know how all these things have worked together to make me what I am,' Charles Dickens wrote later, 'but I never afterwards forgot, I never shall forget, I never can forget, that my mother was warm for my being sent back.' The whole blacking warehouse episode lasted

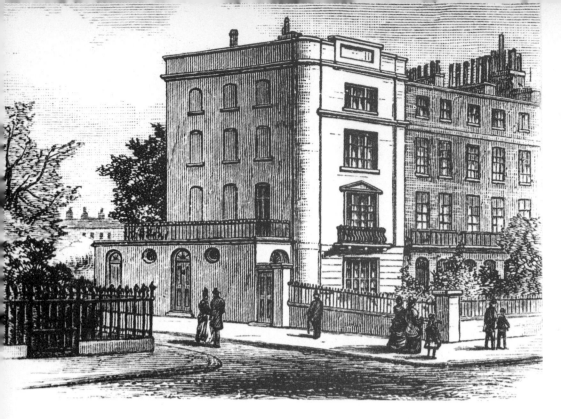

The Wellington House Academy in London

only a few months, but its effect was lasting and profound. Dickens never mentioned it, not even to his wife and children, and his close friend and biographer, John Forster, discovered it only by accident.

One result of the blacking warehouse was that the boy now had a steely determination to succeed. There was to be no sloppy Bohemianism for Charles Dickens, who from now onwards made full use of his extraordinary nervous energy, his equally extraordinary powers of observation, his unusual ability, absent in both his parents, to discipline himself. If there remained in him to the end of his life a certain hard competence, an aggressively sharp efficiency—and Henry James noted his 'military eye'—that was because he never forgot the blacking warehouse and all those tearful visits to the debtors' prison. The happy childhood years in Kent, the dark misery of this London episode, together produced the intense light and shade of his fiction, the bright dream fading into the menacing nightmare. For the next two-and-a-half years he attended the Wellington House Academy, a school with an excellent local reputation. We can discover what he felt there, he who had had experiences very different from anything his schoolfellows had known, from the semi-autobiographical chapters of *David Copperfield*.

A page of
Dickens's shorthand

On leaving school, in 1827, he went as office boy to a firm of solicitors, Ellis and Blackmore, with premises in Raymond Buildings, overlooking Holborn. Now a rather small youth, looking younger than he actually was but carrying himself confidently, with a sharp eye and a very alert manner, Charles Dickens found the law a dull business, but he absorbed so much of its atmosphere and background, noticed so many of its odd figures, that to this day we cannot visit a law office in central London without feeling we are back in the Dickens world. But something much more exciting was offering itself. John Dickens, now pensioned off by the Admiralty, had learnt shorthand and had become one of the parliamentary reporters of the *British Press*. Charles decided to follow his father's example. He too learnt shorthand, a harder task then than it is now,

A court at Doctors' Commons where Dickens worked as a shorthand copyist

especially for a lad in his middle teens at work in an office all day, but he persevered with that determination and self-discipline which marked his character then and afterwards.

Just before his seventeenth birthday he left Ellis and Blackmore, to become a free-lance reporter, sharing a box with a distant relative, at Doctors' Commons, an ancient muddle of many courts, dealing with Admiralty, wills and probate, and ecclesiastical business, in premises situated between St Paul's and the river. (It was abolished in 1857.) But the work was tedious and paid him badly. He had now fallen in love with the daughter of a banker, a pretty little coquette called Maria Beadnell, and in his impatience with his slow progress he turned to the Theatre, for which he had a passion, had some lessons in acting and spent a lot of time learning suitable parts and training himself to perform them. He went to the length of asking for an audition at Covent Garden, but when the day arrived he was prevented from going by a severe cold.

Literature owes much to this cold, for Dickens was a born actor and if he had kept this appointment he might well have been engaged by Mathews and Charles Kemble and then have spent the rest of his life on the stage. As it was,

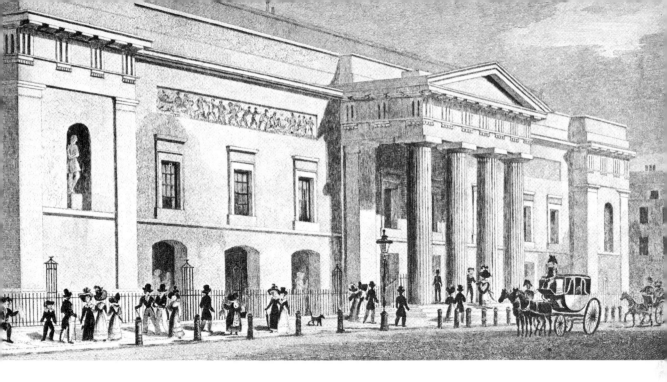

The Theatre Royal, Covent Garden

his prospects as a reporter suddenly improved. His uncle, John Henry Barrow, had started a paper called the *Mirror of Parliament*, for which John Dickens now worked. Charles was invited to join the staff. But in addition, early in this same year, 1832, he was also invited to join the general reporting staff of a new evening paper, the *True Sun*. He was in the Gallery of the House of Commons during the final debates on the Reform Bill. Very soon he was recognised to be one of the fastest and most accurate reporters in the Gallery—or indeed in the whole country. Finally, he became the star reporter on the *Morning Chronicle*, a Liberal daily.

When the House was not sitting, he was sent to cover by-elections, important public meetings in the provinces, banquets and other ceremonious occasions, often working at high speed and travelling as fast as horses would carry him in the hope of delivering his copy before *The Times* reporters could deliver theirs. These spirited dashes about the country were very much to the taste of young Charles Dickens, himself now a very dashing young man, somewhat over-dressed. But all this rich experience, first among the lawyers, then in the House, then at these various provincial elections and functions, was soon to be of great

Dickens as a young man, aged 18

value to the novelist. It has often been said, chiefly by lawyers and politicians, that Dickens did not understand Law and Politics, and was content merely to offer gross caricatures of legal and political figures and proceedings. That he was not deeply concerned with underlying principles is true enough. But these critics forget how much first-hand experience he had had as a reporter, the innumerable hours he had spent filling notebooks with verbatim reports of speeches that were largely humbug and bosh. He had been, so to speak, in the kitchen where the unsavoury messes were cooked. As David Copperfield said: 'Night after night I record predictions that never come to pass, professions that are never fulfilled, explanations that are only meant to mystify. I wallow in words. . . . I am sufficiently behind the scenes to know the worth of political life.' That he often over-simplified, exaggerated, allowed his grotesque humour too much latitude, we cannot deny. But nobody who is not in love with the English Establishment can fail to recognise the truth and the force, the original-ity and significance, of the legal and political satire in Dickens. As a young

A caricature of a
London 'penny theatre'

reporter he may have had no deep personal interest in these matters—though
then and later he had some strong political convictions—but this was a young
man with a very sharp eye and a very keen ear, who knew only too well how
much pompous rubbish was emptied out every day, how many offices and
platforms were occupied by important and expensive noodles. And, when
allowances are made for some changes in manner and style, much of his satire
still strikes home to this day.

These years in London gave him something else—a truly remarkable knowledge of the city and its life on all social levels except the grandest. This his
acquaintances acknowledged. Young Dickens, with his restless energy and
illimitable curiosity, went everywhere and noticed everything, his power of
observation and memory being phenomenal. Although we associate him as a
novelist with London, he had in fact no particular affection for the city, and
later in life declared that he detested it. But from the first he had a passion, which
never entirely left him, for exploring it, and these explorations gave him a

George Hogarth
Dickens's father-in-law

wealth of material for his fiction. On the other hand, his private life during these years brought him little happiness, and this largely accounts for his growing ambition and the almost feverish energy he put into his work. First, his father began drifting towards disaster again, until finally Charles had to make himself responsible for the whole family. Secondly—and more important—he remained violently in love with pretty little Maria Beadnell, who behaved badly, sometimes responding, at other times being coldly aloof, probably encouraged by her family. In the end, weary of being humiliated so often, realising that the capricious and flirtatious Maria was not for him, he put a sudden stop to his long and desperate courtship. Something much more than mere calf love was involved here. Dickens was in terrible earnest, and the girl's quick changes of mood, her tantrums and deceptions, brought him real suffering. That his feeling for her went very deep indeed is proved by the fact that many years later, in his middle age, an unexpected letter from her produced in him an almost uncontrollable excitement. (Their meeting afterwards proved a sharp disappointment, as we know from his parody of it in *Little Dorrit*, very funny

The old Reading Room in the British Museum, where Dickens continued his education

but savage and merciless—he should have written it, for his own sake, and then torn it up, for her sake and perhaps ours.) And the effect of this sadly tormenting first love, both on his life and his work, was very considerable.

It explains why he forced himself to believe that he was in love with Catherine Hogarth, the daughter of a fellow journalist, and why he made a marriage that he must have known was disastrous years before he put an end to it. And this tantalising image of Maria, associated in his mind with so much humiliation and suffering, also helps to explain his unsatisfactory treatment of love in all but the last novels, his avoidance of real sexual passion, his trick of merely prettifying it or making it grotesque. Wild humour, of the sort we find in a Dickens or a Gogol, is often itself a desperate means of escape. It was partly the hidden sexual romantic in Dickens who complained of 'something wanting'. A further result of this passion for the fickle Maria Beadnell, which consumed nearly four years of his life, was that its failure hardened and toughened him, at least outwardly. The energy released by his decision to pursue her no longer went into his work and to raising his own social status. The Beadnell

21

Playbill for the Dickens' amateur theatricals
at his parents' home in 1833

Dickens posting his first literary composition

family had looked down on him. He would show the Beadnells and all like them what Charles Dickens could do.

But what could he do, outside his astonishingly fast accurate reporting? The answer came towards the end of 1833, when he might have been seen paying half-a-crown for the current issue of the *Monthly Magazine*. He held it with a shaking hand; he stared at it with eyes blazing with excitement and afterwards filling with tears. There, secure and glorious for ever in print, was one of his Sketches—*A Dinner In Poplar Walk*. Charles Dickens had begun his literary career. He contributed other pieces to this *Monthly Magazine*, for though it did not pay for such contributions it was a good shop window. He wrote similar things for the new *Evening Chronicle* and *Bell's Life in London*. He used various pseudonyms but the one he used most was the family nursery name of a brother—*Boz*. And now *Boz* began to be talked about. The dashing young Harrison Ainsworth, already making a hit with his historical-cum-crime

London Bridge in Dickens's time

William Harrison Ainsworth
who introduced Dickens
to his first publisher

novels, invited *Boz* Dickens to his Sunday afternoon parties at Kensal Lodge, Willesden. It was there that Dickens met the publisher Macrone, and it was he who suggested that Dickens should assemble his *Boz* Sketches for publication in two volumes, to be illustrated by Cruikshank, then at the height of his reputation. For the copyright of the first edition, Macrone undertook to pay £150. This is worth mentioning if only because too many people assume that young authors nowadays are much better off than they were when Dickens was young. But £150 in 1836 would buy as much as £1,000 will buy in 1961, and no publisher today would offer anything like £1,000 to a young author for a miscellaneous collection of sketches, essays, short tales.

Sketches by Boz appeared in February 1836, and was warmly received. A second edition came out in August, and two more the following year. The descriptive pieces, as distinct from the tales, represent Dickens the reporter and

Title-page for the *Sketches by Boz*

The Pawnbroker's Shop;
a London scene from
Sketches by Boz

sharp observer, not Dickens the novelist and creator, whose towns and streets, taverns and houses, seem to have an extra and fantastic dimension. Apart from a rather forced youthful facetiousness, they are excellent accounts of the London of William IV, and as such can still be enjoyed today.

But now the novelist of genius was to have his chance. A new firm of publishers, Chapman and Hall, had under contract a popular comic artist called Seymour, who specialised in sporting scenes. They wanted some sort of humorous text, describing sporting misadventures (a familiar theme), to support the drawings, and had already tried to interest several well-known humorists in the project but without success. Now Dickens was approached. Would he be willing to write twelve thousand words a month, for twenty monthly parts? He said he would, but only on his own terms. These were that the drawings must illustrate the text, not the text the drawings. In other words, it must be his story, not Seymour's. The publishers, probably impressed by the

A sketch of Dickens
by George Cruikshank, 1836

cool self-confidence of this young writer of twenty-four, finally gave way. Seymour protested of course, but too much time had been wasted trying to find a writer and the artist had to agree. As for Dickens, as he said later: 'I thought of Mr Pickwick.'

The first instalment of *The Pickwick Papers* was advertised to appear at the end of March 1836. Dickens, still working as a reporter, had now to deliver twelve thousand words a month. Something must now be said about this publication in monthly parts, which was standard practice with Dickens throughout his career. Clearly the practice had its dangers, favouring a hand-to-mouth improvisation, a loose narrative and a sprawling wide scene, and certain repetitive tricks that enabled the reader to identify characters quickly and easily. It might be argued—and indeed it often has been argued—that as a creator of literature the novelist had nothing to gain and everything to lose by adopting this method. But this is not true. It may have discouraged careful

The first meeting of the
'Pickwick Club', one of
Seymour's illustrations

planning. It may have encouraged hasty changes in the story or its characters because the parts were not going well. (For example, Martin Chuzzlewit was sent to America to give the story a new interest it needed.) Nevertheless, with a writer like Dickens, so fertile, inventive, marvellously creative, there was probably more gain than loss. This serial publication, with readers eagerly awaiting the next part, stimulated and inspired him, compelled him to work at a speed and with an urgency that released the unconscious elements on which genius depends. A coldly planned and carefully written *Pickwick* would never have been the triumphant comic fairy tale it turned out to be. The sheer necessity of getting it done, month after month, really brought the tale its magic, just because the youthful Dickens had no time to think, to wonder if he was making a fool of himself, but had to be audaciously creative.

Oddly enough, the first few numbers of *Pickwick* made no great stir, selling only a few hundred copies. Moreover, the artist Seymour, a sick and defeated

Pickwick on the Ice;
an illustration by *Phiz*

man, committed suicide, and it was not easy to find a successor. The final choice, Hablôt Knight Browne, who came to sign his illustrations *Phiz*, was even younger than Dickens. The two worked together, generally in the friendliest fashion, for many years, and indeed it is hard to dissociate the earlier Dickens novels from their *Phiz* illustrations. These have their merits, but possibly Browne's fondness for drawing enormously fat and grotesquely thin characters strengthened the belief, held in some superior quarters, that Dickens himself was a caricaturist.

At the end of the fourth number of *Pickwick*, Sam Weller made his appearance, and from then on the public interest and the sales increased rapidly. Long before the twentieth and last number came out, the country was Pickwick mad. The name was given to all manner of things, from coats and hats to canes and cigars. Everybody recognised at a glance the figures of Pickwick and Sam Weller. Their remarks were widely quoted, as indeed they have been ever since.

The soon-to-be-famous trial scene, Bardell *v.* Pickwick, which was Dickens's revenge for all the hours of boredom and disgust he had had to spend in law courts, delighted everybody except the lawyers. The uproarious humour hardly flagged, although there was a new depth, together with some touches of pathos, in the later numbers, notably those in which the debtors' prison was described. The huge rollicking tale could not have appeared at a better time. Scott was dead, and clever young bloods like Bulwer-Lytton, Harrison Ainsworth, Disraeli, clearly were not going to take his place. What was needed was a novelist who would appeal equally to all classes of readers, and Dickens did.

This immense popularity, which he achieved in his middle twenties, he kept for the rest of his life, though of course some novels were liked better than others. It was the kind of popularity quite out of the reach of any novelist nowadays, simply because a writer now has to compete for the time, attention, applause of the biggest public with films, radio and television. The Victorians had none of these distractions; they wanted family entertainment, and in Dickens they had a superb family entertainer. To the very last, when he was a long way from the high-spirited young man of the 1830's, Dickens gladly accepted the fact that he was a family entertainer—though of course he knew that he was a great deal more than that—and tried to provide his family audiences with all they wanted, boisterous humour for Father, sentiment and pathos for Mother and the girls, satire for the cleverer young men. And this was not pot-boiling but the acceptance of what he sincerely believed to be a personal responsibility. He was the public's favourite, its 'inimitable Boz', and worked like a demon continuously to justify this reputation.

Very soon he was equally famous abroad, especially in America and in Russia, where he was translated early and had a great influence on Russian fiction. Indeed, in some respects his genius was more soundly appreciated abroad than at home, where the victims of his satire tried to dismiss him as a mere caricaturist, and superior persons, for whose taste he was altogether too robust and popular, refused to take him seriously as a novelist. (For example, compare Santayana's glowing tribute to him, in *Soliloquies in England*, with Leslie Stephen's grudging faint praise in his Dickens article in the *Dictionary of National Biography*.)

Meanwhile, the astonishing success of *Pickwick* brought about his resignation from the staff of the *Morning Chronicle*. He had now done with reporting but immediately took on a multitude of new commitments, some of them, and those the least successful, concerned with the Theatre, for which he had a passion but, curiously enough, no marked talent as a writer. (But much of his earlier fiction is intensely theatrical in manner and tone, and Dickens's ability as an actor cannot be questioned.) There is no space here for any adequate account of

The Eatanswill by-election, from *The Pickwick Papers*

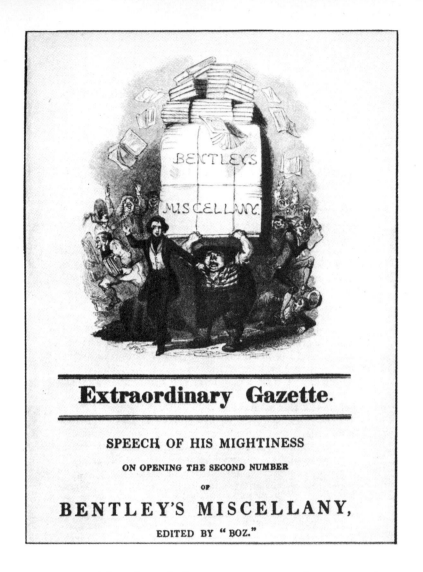

Extraordinary Gazette.

SPEECH OF HIS MIGHTINESS

ON OPENING THE SECOND NUMBER

OF

BENTLEY'S MISCELLANY,

EDITED BY "BOZ."

A prospectus for
Bentley's Miscellany

Dickens's multifarious activities, at this time or later; it is enough to say that his demonic energy, possibly the result of dangerous deep pressures, drove him to accept sufficient work to keep three men going. He accepted an invitation from Bentley, the publisher, to edit a new monthly magazine, called *Bentley's Miscellany*. In it his new novel, *Oliver Twist*, came out as a serial. He arranged with Chapman and Hall to follow *Pickwick* with another long novel to be published in parts—*Nicholas Nickleby*.

He was now a married man, for he and Catherine (Kate) Hogarth were married quietly in Chelsea early in April 1836. They had a week's honeymoon,

Mary Hogarth, Dickens's young sister-in-law   Mrs Charles Dickens in 1836

all he could spare time for, in a small village near Chatham, and then, having no house, settled in his rooms in Furnival's Inn. Kate's younger sister, Mary, a good-looking and charming girl of sixteen, lived with them and continued to live with them when they moved to a house in Doughty Street. The sisters were devoted to each other, and Mary adored Dickens and was probably more responsive to his changing moods, his high spirits and low, than the more lethargic and less quick-witted Kate. There was nothing wrong with Kate, certainly not in these early days, but it was impossible for her to be happily mated with a tempestuous and mercurial man of genius. For another kind of man she might have made an excellent wife. Married to Dickens it was as if she had been tied to the tail of a comet. And a too rapid succession of pregnancies, during these early years, did not help her to face the situation in which she found herself. As for Dickens, although he genuinely believed that he was in love with her when they married and that he loved her for many years afterwards, he was probably deceiving himself. He needed somebody to console himself with after his painful and disastrous pursuit of Maria Beadnell, whose

'Oliver asks for more'

Cruikshank's frontispiece to
Oliver Twist

A drawing by Maclise of
Dickens with his wife
and Mary Hogarth

image he projected on to poor Kate Hogarth. The marriage was probably unsatisfactory from the first, and this would explain Dickens's restlessness, his
demonic energy, his eagerness to undertake an appalling amount of work,
together with his new interest in gadding about in society, his riding and
walking and masculine high jinks. Happy young husbands rarely behave in
this fashion.

Not long after they had moved to Doughty Street, Mary Hogarth, returning
in high spirits from the theatre with Kate and Charles, was suddenly taken ill
(it was probably a heart attack), and the following afternoon she died in
Dickens's arms. For the first time since he turned author he found it impossible
to continue writing, and both *Pickwick* and *Oliver Twist*, then appearing in
monthly instalments, had to be postponed. The sudden death of this seventeen-
year-old girl—'the peace and life of our home', he wrote, 'the admired of all for
her beauty and excellence'—was a cruel calamity from which Dickens perhaps
never really recovered. He wore her ring for the rest of his life. She remained

Angela Burdett-Coutts
aristocrat, philanthropist
and friend of Dickens

in his mind an idealised figure of youth and promise, beauty and charm, cruelly struck down. The death-bed scenes in which he luxuriated probably offered him some release for feelings that he tried to hide from all but his closest friends. His imagination was haunted for years by this figure of bright but tragically doomed youth. And it was probably the loss of Mary Hogarth, piling up emotion outside the reach of any mature woman, that made him so vulnerable in middle age, as we shall see, to the appeal of another young girl, Ellen Ternan.

He was deeply hurt, and remained so even after stopping work and going away for a time, but he was soon busy enlarging his circle of friends and acquaintances. The philanthropic heiress, Miss Burdett-Coutts, became one

Sydney Smith   Robert Lytton, son of Edward Bulwer-Lytton

of his closest friends. He joined other young writers in the semi-literary *salon* of
Lady Blessington and Count D'Orsay. Through Bulwer-Lytton, he was
invited to dine at Holland House, where he met the formidable Macaulay and
the enchanting Sydney Smith and contrived to please that old dragon of Whig
hostesses, Lady Holland herself. He exchanged visits with old Samuel Rogers,
who was kind to Kate though he never invited her to one of his breakfasts.
And a new friendship arrived just when it was most needed; for Dickens,
increasingly successful every month, was now in a tangle of agreements, argu-
ments and quarrels with publishers and badly needed somebody to advise him,
to perform the services any good literary agent would offer a successful author
nowadays. This new friend, John Forster, was full of advice and eager helpful-
ness.

Forster was a little younger than Dickens though he appeared to be much
older. Originally a barrister, he turned to journalism, was dramatic critic of
the *Examiner*, which he edited later, and wrote some historical and literary
biographies, including—his last work—the standard life of Dickens himself.

D. Maclise R.A.
Andi . May 22. 1840

John Forster, Dickens's life-long friend

He was a worthy man, entirely conscientious and sincere, a staunch good friend, who happened to have some unfortunate mannerisms. He had a great admiration for the tragedian Macready, and unconsciously imitated his theatrical gestures and deep solemn tone. He had little tact, a very loud voice, and was extremely opinionated and dogmatic. The inevitable result was that he made many enemies, and may have made some too for Dickens when he acted for him. But there can be no doubt about Dickens's dependence on Forster's judgment and help, which ranged from negotiating with publishers to passing proofs. It is unlikely that he had no influence whatever on Dickens's work, especially the earlier work. (He hardly understood what Dickens was trying to do in the later novels.) His biography is conscientious and solid and it is not Forster's fault, pledged as he was to secrecy and writing as he did shortly after Dickens's death, that too much is left out of it.

We have many accounts of Dickens's appearance and manner during this time of triumph. After turning author he let his hair grow long, so that it curled, almost girlishly, round his smooth cheeks. But in spite of these locks and his dandified velvet coats and waistcoats, he was anything but effeminate in manner or appearance. 'What a face is his to meet in a drawing room!' wrote

Charles Dickens at the height of his fame painted by Maclise ▶

Thomas Carlyle as a young man   Jane Carlyle, his wife

old Leigh Hunt. 'It has the life and soul in it of fifty human beings.' And Jane Carlyle said of his face: 'It was as if made of steel.' A girl who saw much of him at Broadstairs, which he was fond of visiting during these years, has left us an account of the power and magnetism of his brilliant eyes, flashing quick glances that many contemporaries noted. After their first meeting, in 1840, Carlyle, a hard man to please and apt to patronise even when pleased, observed: 'He is a fine little fellow—Boz, I think: clear blue intelligent eyes that he arches amazingly, large protrusive, rather loose mouth, a face of the most utmost *mobility*, which he shuttles about—eyebrows, eyes, mouth and all—in a very singular manner while speaking . . . a quiet, shrewd-looking little fellow, who seems to guess pretty well what he is and what others are.' Even then Dickens could be dictatorial and masterful when he felt he needed to be—and he had an almost military passion for order and tidiness—but he quickly relaxed in genial company, was a wonderful guest at picnics or children's parties, being ready to sing comic songs, conjure or clown (he was a marvellous mimic), and if he had a fault, when in high spirits, it was that some of his antics were too boisterous and embarrassing. Like some other artists associated in our minds

A sketch by Maclise of Dickens's house at Devonshire Terrace

with immense conviviality—and Dickens was able to create this atmosphere in any company—he did not really drink very much himself, at least not by hearty Victorian standards. Even if he had wanted it, he could not afford dissipation. He was committed to do too much—novel-writing, article-writing, editing—and late in 1841, after arranging to visit America, he was compelled to undergo an extremely painful operation—the result, he swore, of sitting so long at his desk.

Meanwhile, he had moved from Doughty Street to a much larger house, far more grandly furnished, No. 1 Devonshire Terrace, close to Regents Park. Here he could entertain in the sumptuous manner of the age. Though only a few years had passed, he was now far removed from the boyish reporter of the *Morning Chronicle*. He was elected to the Athenaeum. And when he visited Edinburgh, not only was he given a great public banquet but he was also made a freeman of the city. He was still not thirty years of age.

The novels he published before he visited America can be considered together. With *Pickwick* they form a group, his earlier fiction, and though they are all very different, for Dickens aimed at variety and never tried to repeat his

A view of Broadstairs in the 1840's

successes, they have also much in common. They are *Oliver Twist*, *Nicholas Nickleby*, *The Old Curiosity Shop*, and *Barnaby Rudge*. Following *Pickwick*, *Oliver Twist* was in the sharpest possible contrast to it, dark and sinister and murderous. It satirised savagely both the workings of the old Poor Laws and the semi-starvation methods of the new Act of 1834, and so was the first of Dickens's many and famous attacks on public abuses. Two points need to be made about these attacks. Dickens has often been accused of being too general and vague in his treatment of these abuses, but such criticism overlooks the fact that in the world of his fiction he could not afford to be precise and document-ary, and the further fact that from now onwards he wrote many long articles denouncing these abuses and stating his personal opinion quite clearly. The second point is that too often he has been credited with the discovery of these abuses, when in most instances he was bringing into fiction what many of his readers already knew, giving shape and colour and drama to what were already public scandals.

For example, the Yorkshire schools, pilloried in *Nicholas Nickleby* as Dotheboys Hall, had been notorious for many years. Dickens himself had heard something about them when he was still a child, at Chatham. The actual schools were no better than Dotheboys Hall. They made a mere pretence of educating their wretched pupils, who were of course mostly unwanted children; they underfed them, kept them in appalling conditions, bullied them unmercifully. Before writing *Nicholas Nickleby*, Dickens, accompanied by *Phiz*, went to North Yorkshire, a hard journey then in the depths of winter, to find out everything about these schools for himself, and though he was not very successful, some of the material in the Dotheboys Hall chapters was founded on fact.

This novel, first appearing in monthly parts, repeated the success of *Pickwick*. It shows us Dickens's earlier fiction at its best and at its worst. The humour of Squeers and the Crummles and the Mantalinis is wonderful, well up to the standard of *Pickwick*. The sentimental and melodramatic passages seem to belong to the Theatre of the Crummles, being over-written and unreal, the young

'Dotheboys Hall',
a scene from *Nicholas Nickleby*

A prospectus announcing
Dickens's miscellany
Master Humphrey's Clock

Dickens at his worst. But its humour and lively bustle, its gallery of eccentrics, save this long wandering tale, and it has remained a favourite.

The next novel, *The Old Curiosity Shop*, came out of an attempt on Dickens's part to rescue himself and his publishers, Chapman and Hall, from a disastrous situation. He had persuaded them to let him bring out a weekly miscellany, *Master Humphrey's Clock*, but the sales of the second and third numbers were so disappointing that he was compelled to save the enterprise. The trouble was, the public wanted Dickens but they wanted him as a storyteller in the big rambling style of *Pickwick* and *Nicholas Nickleby*. So the *Clock* had to be filled with the story of Little Nell and her grandfather and their adventures on the road. Much of it was written at Broadstairs, where Dickens would rise early and do a long morning's work. The weekly figures went up and up, and while the story was still being serialised and the final chapters not even written, a

Walter Savage Landor
one of Dickens's
famous admirers

dramatic version of it was being prepared for the Adelphi Theatre. *The Old Curiosity Shop* was an immediate and immense success.

It offered its readers an admirable assortment of characters—Dick Swiveller and the Marchioness, the diabolical Quilp and Sampson Brass and his sister, the Nubbles family and Codlin and Short—but it was Little Nell who en-thralled them. Her death was the most tragic event of the year for the whole English-speaking world. Strong men like Macready the actor-manager, O'Connell the Irish politician, Lord Jeffrey the lawyer and critic, burst into tears. While London was drying its eyes, crowds waiting for the ship from England at the pier in New York cried to the sailors 'Is Little Nell dead?', and then America wept. What modern critics and most readers now regard with distaste could then move deeply men like Landor and Carlyle. What was accepted then as one of Dickens's chief glories, his command of pathos, is now condemned as cheap sentiment and bad taste. The truth is, the Early Victorians, tough people living in a brutal world (where Little Nells were working from daybreak to dark in mines and cotton mills), *wished* to be moved, to luxuriate with their author in long-drawn-out pathos and tears. They felt it did them good. We on our part resent being moved in this fashion, and steel ourselves against an author who is deliberately playing on our feelings. We think that pathos, if there must be any at all, should be brief, sharp, bitter, and death-bed scenes as short as possible, not described to the last detail in page after page of luxuriously mournful prose that begins to read like bad blank verse. It is this change of taste that has reduced *The Old Curiosity Shop*, perhaps Dickens's greatest immediate triumph, to one of his minor and most neglected novels. He himself, while working on it, was as genuinely moved as any of his readers were to be, but on a deeper and less conscious level he was probably determined to rescue his weekly *Clock*, his only failure so far, giving his public a sudden huge dose of what he knew it wanted. To be fair, we must remember that help-less, forlorn, menaced childhood was something he understood only too well.

Little Nell and the Old Man, a scene from *The Old Curiosity Shop*

Washington Irving
the great American writer

The last of this quartet of novels, *Barnaby Rudge*, was one he had been intend-ing to write for several years, and finally had to write in order to fulfil a contract he had with Bentley. His reluctance to settle down to it is significant. He might not be able to drop the idea but it failed to inspire him. The story was set in the past and he was not, and never could be, an historical novelist. The inevitable result was that *Barnaby Rudge* was disappointing. Even the humour, unlike that of *The Old Curiosity Shop*, seemed forced and rather mechanical, that of a writer imitating himself. But the passages based on the Gordon Riots, which come too late and after too much tedious plotting to save the story, are very powerful, and have in them a force and urgency which suggest that something deep in Dickens's divided nature found release in these scenes of dark violence.

With all these four novels off his hands, Dickens now decided to visit America, and spent much of the autumn of 1841 making his plans. There were many good reasons for going to America. He had a large admiring public there. He wanted to meet some American writers, especially Washington Irving, with whom he had exchanged enthusiastic letters. He felt ready to enjoy and

The steamship *Britannia* in which Dickens sailed to America

applaud a truly democratic society. Finally, he was anxious to make a direct appeal to the Americans about copyright. The position was that the United States had never signed the international agreement, with the result that a popular English author like Dickens, though he might have an official American publisher, could not protect his work against being pirated there. Various American editions of his novels might be sold by the hundred thousand, but they would not bring him a penny. (In spite of the protests by Dickens and many other English writers, a number of the best-known American writers, and the more serious American newspapers and periodicals, nothing was done about copyright in Dickens's lifetime. It was nearly the end of the century before America joined the international agreement. Nowadays, the U.S.S.R. behaves more or less as America did in Dickens's time, and similar protests are constantly being made by contemporary authors, who find their work unprotected by copyright in Russia.) Nobody felt more strongly about this situation than Dickens, and he was determined that the Americans should learn directly from him what his feelings were, how much he had lost because his novels had been pirated.

He was to sail early in 1842. Kate did not really want to go, not wishing to be so widely separated from her young family, and probably Dickens should not have insisted upon her accompanying him. The house in Devonshire Terrace was let furnished for six months. An arrangement was made with Chapman and Hall that they should let him have £150 a month in advance of future royalties. Macready and his wife and Dickens's brother Frederick made themselves responsible for the children. After much planning, buying and packing of new clothes, many letters of welcome from America and of farewell good wishes from friends at home, much dining and wining, with Dickens in the highest spirits and Kate in the lowest, they sailed on January 4 in the *Britannia*, a paddle steamer of only 1154 tons. They ran into the North Atlantic at its worst. Dickens was seasick for five days; Kate and her maid were both sick and terrified (as well they might be) and stayed in their berths. After ten days, the weather was so bad, the ship rolling so violently, that Dickens, up

Dickens during the voyage:
a sketch made by a fellow-passenger

and about now, found in the saloon only four out of the total of eighty-six passengers. They arrived at Halifax after sixteen days, stayed there a few hours, then sailed, running into more rough weather, for Boston.

Where Dickens went, what he felt and thought about all he saw, may be found in his *American Notes*. After Boston, he visited New York, Philadelphia, Baltimore (where Poe came to see him), Washington, Pittsburg, Cincinatti, and St Louis, then on to the edge of the untamed Far West. He never went further south than Virginia, but saw enough of slavery to confirm his detestation of it. He had the greatest welcome that probably any visitor to America has ever had. He was lionised and mobbed everywhere. But after Boston and New England, which he admired and liked, he enjoyed himself less and less. There were many reasons for this. There was the increasing discomfort of the travel as they went west, and the rougher manners. (The constant tobacco-chewing and spitting became intolerable.) There was—a circumstance for which he probably did not make enough allowance—the strain of being on view all the time, for though the Americans were ready to admire him and cheer him, they were not willing to let him have some privacy and peace. There was the ugly desolation

A slave-auction in the Deep South

Broadway, New York, at the time of Dickens's visit

of the newer settlements. There was too much aggressive boasting, too much resentment of any criticism. Finally, what was most important, there was the attitude towards him of the popular press, which attacked him viciously because he protested publicly about the absence of copyright protection in America. In spite of these attacks, Dickens, knowing he was in the right, courageously refused to withdraw a word. It may be said, as some of his friends in England did say, that a visitor enjoying such a welcome chose a bad time to ventilate such grievances; but we must remember that the best American writers and newspapers were in solid agreement with him. The screaming opposition came from the less scrupulous publishers and booksellers and the largely ignorant American public that took its opinions from the sensation-hunting cheap press. And though the America of today is very different from the America of the 1840's, it is not hard to discover there now what Dickens liked and disliked then.

Leaving behind him many new good friends, who were to remain his friends to the end of his life, he sailed thankfully for home in June, and was in

Tremont House, where Dickens stayed in Boston

tremendous high spirits throughout the voyage. Making use of the long letters he had sent from America to John Forster and other friends, he began writing his *American Notes* as soon as he was back in his study at Devonshire Terrace, kept at it throughout another stay at Broadstairs, and by autumn the book was finished. It excited nobody in England, but in America, where large pirated editions of it were sold very quickly, it created a sensation. Once again, there was a sharp contrast between responsible opinion and the cheap press, which redoubled its attacks on the author. But now, in 1843, he had other things to worry about. The glorious good fortune of the last six years seemed to be leaving him.

He had a bitter quarrel with Chapman and Hall about money. Bradbury and Evans, the printers, were interested in the idea of publishing him, but nothing as yet had been settled. His father and two of his brothers had to be helped; he was still living in the grand Devonshire Terrace style; and now his earnings were falling. What was worse still, the new novel, *Martin Chuzzlewit*, now coming out in parts, was selling badly. It picked up a little when Martin, as we have already noticed, was packed off to America, enabling Dickens, in chapters of wild but very funny burlesque, to counter-attack all the American

Douglas Jerrold, friend
and admirer of Dickens

journalists who had been abusing him. The glorious Sairey Gamp was an immediate success. But the novel as a whole could not be conjured into a popular favourite.

It is in fact a transition piece between his improvised fun-and-melodrama earlier fiction and the planned and solid later novels. Unlike the earlier tales it has a central theme—selfishness. It has an elaborately involved plot structure, to which it owes some incredible incidents but also a few scenes of great power. Its chief weakness is that its sympathetic characters tend to be dull and rather lifeless, and its villainous characters are too comic or grotesque to play the parts allotted to them by the plot. Mr Pecksniff, for example, is a wonderful comic creation, but we cannot be expected to take him seriously in the Chuzzlewit story. Like Mrs Gamp and Mrs Todgers, he exists in another kind of world, one quite removed from any drama of moral values. Dickens had either to subdue his natural exuberance, creating gigantic grotesques and uproarious comedy, or to abandon any idea of a central theme and a complicated story to illustrate it. He could not criticise this world if he was still at the same time creating a comic elfland. This, as *Martin Chuzzlewit* plainly shows, was his dilemma.

Two more friends of Dickens: Macready, the great actor, and Thackeray the novelist

But he escaped from it temporarily by suddenly deciding to write a fantasy about Christmas. Never had he worked before with such furious energy and enthusiasm, with so much laughter and so many tears, as he did on *A Christmas Carol*. And the public soon shared his enthusiasm, laughed and cried with him: this *Carol*, the first of his Christmas Books, remained a popular favourite, to be read aloud after the plum pudding and mince pies had been eaten, for years after his death. That Dickens could celebrate the season hilariously in reality and not only in imagination, we know from contemporary accounts of parties he gave or attended. Of one, at this very time, a children's party at the Macreadys', Jane Carlyle records: 'Dickens and Forster above all exerted themselves till the perspiration was pouring down and they seemed *drunk* with their efforts. Only think of that excellent Dickens playing the *conjuror* for one whole hour—the *best* conjuror I ever saw . . . *after supper* when we were all madder than ever with the pulling of crackers, the drinking of champagne, and the making of speeches; a universal country dance was proposed. . . .'

A scene from an early stage version of the *Christmas Carol*

Thackeray was there, roaring with laughter, and that night the two great novelists were probably closer to a real friendship than they ever were before or afterwards.

The new year, 1844, however, brought its troubles. The *Carol* had been published for Dickens on commission by Chapman and Hall. He had insisted that the book, well-bound and illustrated, should be sold for only five shillings, with the result that its success did not bring him anything like the profit he had been expecting. He was now really short of money. Moreover, although he won a troublesome action against unscrupulous publishers who were bringing out obvious plagiarisms of his work, he received no damages because they went bankrupt, and was several hundred pounds out of pocket. He was anxious now to live abroad, giving the reason that it would be much cheaper to bring up a growing family in France or Italy, especially in Italy. This was true, but it does not altogether explain why he wanted to go. He felt restless and no longer quite at home in London. Advice poured in about where he should go. Friends

A street-scene in
Genoa in the 1840's

living abroad suggested this place and that, an Italian palazzo here, a villa there. In the end a villa in Albaro, just outside Genoa, was rented for three months. For the journey there Dickens bought, for £45, an enormous old coach, in which the whole party travelled across France and then by sea from Marseilles to Genoa. There were Charles and Kate Dickens, Kate's young sister Georgina, four children whose ages ranged from two-and-a-half to seven-and-a-half years, three women servants and a French courier.

Georgina Hogarth was now a member of the Dickens household. She had seen a great deal of the children, who were devoted to her, while their parents were away in America, and perhaps it was the children who demanded that 'Aunt Georgy' should remain with them. She was about the same age that Mary Hogarth had been at the time of her death, and she looked like Mary.

The *Palazzo Peschiere* in Genoa

This probably helped Dickens to release himself from the bonds of sentimental attachment to his dead sister-in-law. Kate, who could be very jealous, raised no objection to Georgina's making her home with them, though later she resented the way in which Georgina took charge of everything. After the separation, as we shall see, Georgina remained with Dickens, to continue looking after the family and the house. This produced a certain amount of scandalous talk, but there is no evidence at all that there was any sexual relationship between Dickens and his sister-in-law. Indeed, both before and after his death, Georgina was very friendly with his mistress, Ellen Ternan. Having grown up with the Dickenses and their family, being quick and competent where her sister Kate was slow and incompetent, being depended upon by all the children, Georgina naturally stayed on and did the work she felt best fitted to do. As she grew up to be extremely able and responsible, this meant that the ever-restless Dickens could leave home with an easy conscience.

The villa in Albaro was a disappointment, and after the three months were up Dickens moved into the magnificent *Palazzo Peschiere*, in Genoa itself. He loved the blazing sunlight, the colour, the cheerful bustle, the warm humanity of the ordinary Italian people, but found it hard to work in Genoa, with its endless clashing and clanging of bells. He sadly missed his long night walks in

Dickens reading *The Chimes* to his friends in London

London, which brought him ideas he could use in his work. For some months he wrote nothing, but then the bells of Genoa suggested a possible Christmas Book for 1844, to be called *The Chimes*. He devised a story that would set in sharp contrast the figure of a humble little porter and the cold hard theories of the economists, and in the autumn he set to work on it with enthusiasm.

Meanwhile, an odd situation developed. A neighbour, a Swiss banker called De La Rue, had an English wife who suffered from some nervous trouble and recurring nightmares. Dickens discovered that he was able to afford Mrs De La Rue some relief by hypnotising her, with the result that he was called in at all hours, often in the middle of the night, to charm away her nightmares and fears. He was entirely serious about this, much to Kate's disquiet, for she was sceptical about this hypnotism, did not trust little Mrs De La Rue, even if the Swiss husband did, and saw in these midnight visits the beginnings of an affair. It is likely that Mrs De La Rue was more than half in love with Dickens, but it was as a hypnotist and witch-doctor, not as a man and a lover, that he himself was involved in these curious proceedings.

As soon as he had finished *The Chimes*, Dickens arranged that he should give a reading of it to his friends in London, early in December. (When we

A carnival in Rome in the 1840's

remember the slowness, expense, discomfort, of travel in the 1840's, we can only wonder what the restless Dickens would have done in our present age of jet flights.) He did not go straight to London but made a little tour of North Italy, ending at Venice, where he was fascinated by the beauty of the place and appalled by its old dungeons and torture chambers. The reading, given in Forster's chambers to a small company of men, was such a marked success that it had to be repeated, a few nights later. The public readings that Dickens gave afterwards owed something to this experiment. He had a great deal of the actor in him, and loved the direct response of an audience. The close attention, the laughter and tears, the applause, the excitement, helped him to forget for a while his restless unhappiness, his sense of 'a want of something'.

He returned to Genoa in time to spend Christmas with his family. The news of *The Chimes* was good, twenty thousand copies having been sold, bringing him already about £1,500. Later, he went with Kate to Pisa, Leghorn, Siena and Rome, and then down to Naples, where they were joined by Georgy, who had come by sea. They returned to Rome for Holy Week, and there the De La Rues turned up, Mrs De La Rue urgently requiring more treatment. On the way back to Genoa, the party, which now included the De La Rues,

Florence, visited by Dickens during his first Italian tour

stayed in Florence, where Lord and Lady Holland, who had a villa there, gave a reception so that the English residents, which included Mrs Trollope (herself a writer and the mother of the novelist), could meet Dickens. When they got back to Genoa, Kate was no longer speaking to the De La Rues, and Dickens, for the first but not the last time, had to pretend that his wife suffered from severe attacks of nerves.

Dickens now planned his *Pictures from Italy*, to be published by Bradbury and Evans, with illustrations by Samuel Palmer. There is nothing of his highly individual genius in these travel sketches. He was the wrong man to write about Italy. He had little feeling for art; his sense of the past was weak; he lacked the background of knowledge to appreciate to the full what he saw on his Italian travels. Lesser men have written far better books on this same subject. *Pictures from Italy* is Early Victorian journalism. Dickens's powers of observation were superb, but they had to be used in the service of his intensely creative imagination, to bring masses of credible and impressive detail to the unique world he created in his fiction. Writing a travel book, especially on a country like Italy so rich in art and history, he was working outside his genius.

A programme for
Every Man in his Humour,
with portrait sketches of
Dickens and Forster
in costume

Returning to London and Devonshire Terrace, in the summer of 1845, after being a year away, Dickens plunged at once into almost every kind of activity except the supremely important one of writing novels. One of these activities was amateur theatricals, which gave him a chance not only to act but also to stage-manage and, indeed, to manage generally, persuading and bullying his friends in the cast, tearing around doing six things at once. The play chosen was Ben Jonson's *Every Man in His Humour*, in which Dickens played Bobadil, and two performances were given for charity, the second in a larger theatre and before a grand and glittering audience. Until he took to giving public readings, turning himself, so to speak, into a one-man theatrical company, these amateur productions offered him just the outlet he needed. They

A cartoon which appeared when Dickens started the *Daily News*

began as a lark among friends, with preliminary discussion of them a good excuse for dining and wining, but then, as rehearsals proceeded and the opening night drew nearer, they were regarded with increasing seriousness, certainly by Dickens, who thought about nothing else at such times. When his astonishing energy was not being controlled by the necessity of working on a big novel, he had to find outlets for it somehow. It was impossible for him to live quietly within himself. Feeling insecure, dissatisfied, often downright unhappy, he had to be either working hard or playing hard.

Now comes what is probably the strangest episode in Dickens's working life. He spent the later months of 1845 secretly and almost feverishly making plans to publish a radical-cum-Liberal newspaper, to be called the *Daily News*. He raised the necessary capital. After his own early experience, he knew all about the reporting side, of course, but now he learnt how the foreign news services were run. He began engaging a staff, and as his terms were generous and many of the best journalists in London were among his friends, it was on the whole a very good staff. (But other editors, losing some of their best men, were

The old *Daily News* offices in Fleet Street before demolition

naturally hostile to this venture.) There was nothing wrong with the idea of bringing out such a paper. The time was ripe for it. And indeed the *Daily News* was to have a long and honourable life in English journalism. What was astonishing was that he ever could have believed that he was capable of settling down to the daily routine and the heavy responsibility of editorship. Nevertheless, he had himself appointed as editor at £2,000 a year, and in January 1846, the *Daily News*, edited by Charles Dickens, made its appearance.

Then, almost at once, he talked of resigning, of going abroad to begin a new novel. It is just possible, though not likely, that he had never seriously intended to continue as editor, that he was merely making sure, by lending his name to it, that a daily paper of radical opinion would now be published. But

Lausanne, where Dickens lived in 1847

the months of eager preparation do not suggest this. Moreover, a cool sly move of this kind was quite foreign to Dickens's temperament. The most reasonable explanation is that not knowing what to do with himself, having no story demanding to be written, he rushed into making his newspaper plans and then when they succeeded, when all the fun was over and he found himself condemned to sit in a newspaper office every day, he suddenly lost heart and lost interest. Fortunately, his closest friend, Forster, was an experienced journalist, and was able to take over the responsibility. The *Daily News* continued without Dickens, though he contributed to it some strong denunciations of public executions and of capital punishment in general. 'I beg to be understood', he concluded, 'to advocate the total abolition of the Punishment of Death as a general principle, for the advantage of society. . . .' Here, using his head as well as his heart, he was far in advance of his time. Indeed, his country has not caught up with him yet.

Tired of London, Dickens wanted to take the whole family abroad again. Kate did not object, but she absolutely refused to return to Genoa. They

Daniel Maclise RA,
the friend and
portraitist of Dickens

finally decided on Switzerland and Lausanne, where they rented a pretty little house with a view over the lake. Lausanne had a number of English summer residents, and they asked their friends to visit them, so that Dickens had plenty of social life. In fact he had more than he wanted. He had now begun *Dombey and Son*, to appear in monthly parts. It was hard work. His letters are filled with complaints: too much social life, too many callers; he misses his long nocturnal walks in city streets; the climate is wrong, the weather is against him. There was some truth in all this, but the fact was, *Dombey* was hard work because he could no longer rapidly improvise and because he was trying to write something far more difficult.

He could no longer keep two stories going. This meant that he had to stop *Dombey* to write his Christmas Book—*The Battle of Life*. (His previous one, following *The Chimes*, had been *The Cricket on the Hearth*.) These Christmas Books, which had an increasing sale, pleased his large public and made a useful addition to his income. But stories like *The Battle of Life*, in which he almost burlesqued himself, asked to be condemned by the more serious reviewers, and did his literary reputation a great deal more harm than good.

Victor Hugo
the famous novelist

He would have been well advised not to write any more Christmas Books until he had an idea for one that he could not resist. (He did fail to bring one out the following year.) Concentrating on *Dombey*, his most ambitious novel so far, he was really in no mood to write a good Christmas Book, as *The Battle of Life* suggests only too well.

After six months in Lausanne, Dickens felt that *Dombey* needed the excitement and zest that only a city, with its crowded streets, its theatres, its night life, could give him. So he moved the whole family to Paris, where he found a very odd house in the Faubourg St Honoré: 'Something,' he said, 'between a baby house, a shades, a haunted castle, and a mad kind of clock, and not to be imagined by the mind of man.' Paris was very cold that winter, and the house cost a small fortune in firewood and even then could not be properly warmed. Moreover, he could never find a place in it where he could settle down to write. He went to London just before Christmas to discuss a cheap edition of his novels that would have new prefaces.

A fashionable Paris salon in 1846

But if he found it difficult to write, he was at last free from any anxiety about money. The monthly parts of *Dombey and Son* were selling well, and his earlier books were now earning money again. Whatever troubles might be ahead, financially he had turned a corner, he had no further need to borrow money, he felt reasonably secure. Forster joined him in Paris for a fortnight's holiday, which they spent going to theatres and meeting French authors. The aged Chateaubriand, Lamartine, Dumas, Gautier, Eugène Sue, Scribe, and above all, the great Hugo, for whom Dickens had a particular admiration, were among these writers.

In March 1847, Dickens moved his family back to London, and as the Devonshire Terrace house was still let, he took a furnished house for three months in Chester Place. There he worked hard at *Dombey* during the day, and entertained his friends or dined out most evenings. The summer was spent once again at Broadstairs, though in July Dickens had to take his amateur theatrical troupe to Manchester. By the early autumn they were all back in

A sketch of Dickens and his friends on holiday

Devonshire Terrace again. After Christmas, he went with Kate to Scotland, and had to stay there longer than he had intended because Kate, who had had a miscarriage, had to keep to her bed. Later there were amateur theatricals again, this time to raise money for the curatorship of Shakespeare's house at Stratford-on-Avon. Under Dickens's management, *The Merry Wives of Windsor* was produced, together with some one-act farces. After a performance at the Haymarket Theatre in April, the company visited Manchester, Liverpool, Birmingham, Edinburgh and Glasgow, with Dickens in the highest spirits throughout the tour. There can be no doubt that all this acting, managing, travelling, served as a safety-valve for a dangerous inner high pressure.

Dombey and Son was finished at last. The twenty monthly numbers had gone very well. The death of Paul Dombey had repeated the tearful triumph of Little Nell. Even Thackeray, now bringing out *Vanity Fair* in similar parts, found this death-bed scene irresistible. But though the novel was a success both with the critics and the public, it is doubtful if its significance was fully understood. In his earlier novels Dickens had attacked abuses that all decent

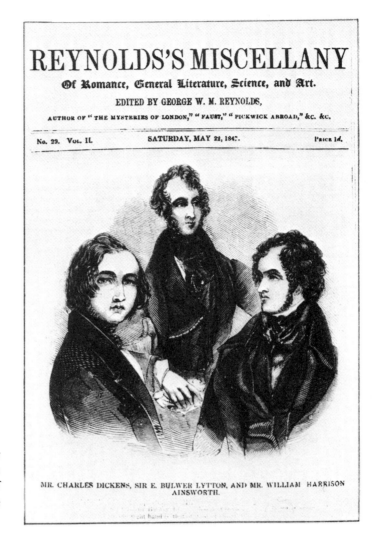

REYNOLDS'S MISCELLANY
Of Romance, General Literature, Science, and Art.
EDITED BY GEORGE W. M. REYNOLDS,
AUTHOR OF "THE MYSTERIES OF LONDON," "FAUST," "PICKWICK ABROAD," &C. &C.

No. 29. Vol. II.   SATURDAY, MAY 22, 1847.   Price 1d.

MR. CHARLES DICKENS, SIR E. BULWER LYTTON, AND MR. WILLIAM HARRISON AINSWORTH.

The three most popular writers in England, as portrayed on the cover of a contemporary magazine

people disliked. And their stories were like melodramas in which good persons were the victims of the wicked. But now, though much of the plot turns on the cold calculating pride of Dombey himself, the chilly selfishness that cuts him off from life, it is a whole section of society, a complete way of living, a familiar attitude of mind, that are examined and denounced. And the contrast between life-denying and life-enhancing attitudes dominates the novel, which swings between characters and scenes that are cold, mechanical, dead, and those that are filled with warmth and life. In spite of its contemporary theme and background, it does not actually represent a move towards realism. It is in its own way a symbolic poetical novel. Everything in it, down to the smallest detail, is

Title-page for *The Haunted Man*. one of the *Christmas Stories*

made to serve its author's main purpose. This is a great advance on his earlier improvisations, no matter how brilliant and entertaining they might be. The man who wrote *Dombey and Son* is now an artist. Dickens the novelist has arrived at his maturity. Superior intellectual contemporaries might prefer, as most of them did, Thackeray's cynical-sentimental chronicle, *Vanity Fair*, to *Dombey and Son*, but in point of fact it is Dickens and not Thackeray who is attempting an important experiment in fiction and leading the way for later novelists. And if, as we know, he found this novel harder to write, it was not really because he suffered from visitors, noise, the weather, and all the other plagues, it was not because there was any real failure of creative power and zest, it was because he was doing something new and difficult.

The next two years were crowded as before with wining and dining, public meetings and banquets (a selection from Dickens's speeches fills a volume),

The first issue of _Household Words_

more amateur theatricals, journeys to and from the seaside; but they also brought him a new and more valuable outlet for his extraordinary nervous energy. Now he became what he continued to be for the rest of his life—a magazine editor. He arranged with Bradbury and Evans to publish a two-penny weekly, of which he would be half-owner. After much discussion, chiefly with Forster, it was called _Household Words_. To which was added: 'Conducted by Charles Dickens.' His was the only name that appeared in the magazine, all the contributions being unsigned. This anonymity was still fairly common in journalism, but it is surprising that Dickens, whose own name appeared at the top of every page, should have followed this practice. He should have realised that in this way he was preventing the young journalists he discovered from making names for themselves. Possibly he felt it would be easier to find and print some articles of strong radical protests, anti-Establishment

The 'Black Country' in early Victorian England

pieces we might call them now, if they could appear without names attached to them. And although *Household Words* offered plenty of entertainment, it was also very much a periodical of radical reform.

It made its first appearance at the end of March 1850, and though it carried no names except that of its 'Conductor' and was not very attractive in appearance, being printed in rather close double-columns, it sold about a hundred thousand copies. It was a success, and remained one. For this all the credit must be given to Dickens, not only because it was his idea, his creation, but also because he turned himself into a conscientious, hard-working and extremely able editor. Wherever he happened to be, he read manuscripts by the score; he corresponded with all manner of contributors; he re-wrote articles that had good matter in them but were not ready for print; he cut and trimmed novels to make them more acceptable as weekly serials. This time there was no question of suddenly losing interest. He edited *Household Words* as if his life depended on it. And perhaps in a sense his life did.

Charles Dickens in 1849

He needed not only an outlet for his energy but also a chance to make good use of his reforming and social crusading zeal. Now that he understood contemporary society better, he knew there was a great deal that was horribly wrong with it. So *Household Words*, week after week, tackled subjects like public health, education, the poor laws, prison reform, emigration, housing, factory conditions, Sunday observance, and offered more good sense on these and similar topics than could be heard in the House of Commons or found in the weighty reviews. What from now on, when he was working at his best, could be treated imaginatively and symbolically in his fiction could be dealt with directly in *Household Words*. The radical reformer in him now had his platform.

It was, however, a popular family magazine, with something for everybody in it and offering plenty of good literary entertainment. Among its contributors were Mrs Gaskell, George Meredith (as a poet), Charles Reade, Coventry Patmore, Sheridan Le Fanu, and Wilkie Collins, soon to be one of Dickens's closest friends. A number of young journalists, men like George Augustus

Wilkie Collins

Sala, Edmund Yates, James Payn, referred to as 'Dickens's young men', began their careers with his encouragement and help. There was now a new reading public, as Dickens knew from his travels up and down the country, a public willing to read about much-needed reforms at home, or the Californian Gold Rush and whale-hunting, eager for both instruction and entertainment; and *Household Words* gave this public exactly what it wanted. But we must remember, now that this last phrase has an ugly ring, that what this public wanted was what Dickens also wanted. His genius apart, he was a member of it. He was not cynically cajoling money out of a lot of half-wits. He saw his readers not as so many units of circulation but as men and brothers. That is why he can be regarded as the great pioneer of the new journalism so long as we understand that he was a pioneer with a difference. There was a great deal now that he was ready to denounce and reject, but he still believed passionately in the kind of

An illustration from *David Copperfield*

ordinary people who wished to learn, to understand, to enjoy, to take a larger hold on life. And for them he toiled, conducting *Household Words*.

At the time this weekly magazine first appeared, *David Copperfield* was coming out in monthly parts, illustrated by *Phiz*. They began in May 1849 and ended in November 1850, when Dickens wrote: 'It would concern the reader little perhaps, to know how sorrowfully the pen is laid down at the close of a two-years' imaginative task; or how an Author feels as if he were dismissing some portion of himself into the shadowy world, when a crowd of the creatures of his brain are going from him for ever.' He ended a preface to a later edition as follows: 'It will be easily believed that I am a fond parent to every child of my fancy, and that no one can ever love that family as dearly as I love them. But, like many fond parents, I have in my heart of hearts a favourite child. And his name is DAVID COPPERFIELD.' For many years, long after Dickens's death, both critical and popular opinion shared his view of this novel. It was held to be his supreme masterpiece. If it has fallen from favour in recent years, that is chiefly because of the new critical interest in the structure

David Copperfield
meeting his aunt

and significance of the later novels, from *Bleak House* onwards. *David Copperfield* belongs to no group of works, has no companions in his fiction, cannot be compared with any other of his novels: whether it is his masterpiece or not even one of his most important works, it stands by itself.

Before he had thought of *David Copperfield*, while he was wondering what to do next, after *Dombey and Son* was off his hands, his friend and adviser, Forster, suggested that the new novel might be a story told in the first person. It happened that Dickens had already written in secret some chapters of autobiography. It also happened that various events round about this time brought painful remainders of his early life. So *David Copperfield* was born. But it is far from being—as many novels have been—so much autobiography dressed up as fiction. There is in it an elaborate and often subtle transmutation. For instance,

David Copperfield
and the kind-hearted
publican's wife

Dickens's father and mother are not present in the novel as whole characters; various aspects of them are divided among various characters. Again, David Copperfield's adventures in childhood and youth are not Dickens's, but on the other hand both have the same psychological and emotional basis. David's first marriage, to the childish Dora, represents old daydreams, first remembered and then critically considered: it is what *might* have happened if young Dickens had had his way and had married Maria Beadnell. Throughout this novel there is a very complicated delicate relation between autobiography and fiction, what has been remembered and what has been invented.

It was the first favourite for so long probably because it has more charm than any other of Dickens's novels. As pieces of writing the early chapters are unquestionably the best. This is the world of childhood as few novelists anywhere

A popular dance
was named after
David Copperfield

have been able to capture it. Dickens is a poet here. He is also an innovator in highly subjective narrative, and for this, even now, he has not been given sufficient credit. As far as the first third of the book is concerned, we are ready to join in the praise and applause of his contemporaries. This account of David's childhood is indeed a masterpiece. But the last third of the book, with David an adult, does not make us laugh (in spite of the glorious Micawbers) and cry and marvel, as it did earlier readers. We feel that the magic has gone, that there is a falling off even by the usual standards of good fiction. The action is forced and incredible. Once out of the nightmares and enchantments of childhood, David is rather a dull young man. It is not that these later chapters are really

The amateur performance of *Not so Bad as We Seem* before the Royal Family at the Duke of Devonshire's London home

bad Dickens, but they seem to us now a descent and a disappointment after those wonderful early passages. We cannot enjoy it all as much as his contemporary readers and he himself did.

While *David Copperfield* was still coming out in parts, Dickens was busy planning, with Bulwer-Lytton, a Guild of Literature and Art, a well-meaning but not very workable scheme for housing and keeping aged or sick authors. There were performances in Lytton's banqueting hall at Knebworth, by Dickens and his troupe, to raise money for the Guild. But something more ambitious was planned for 1851, the year of the Great Exhibition. Dickens and his friends, now including Wilkie Collins and Augustus Egg the painter, would act in a new play by Lytton—*Not So Bad As We Seem*. So now there were more theatricals, on a grander scale, with the Duke of Devonshire as a patron and host, and afterwards a triumphal tour of the provinces. How Dickens contrived to do all this acting and managing and travelling, with

Tavistock House before it was demolished

novels to write and a weekly magazine to edit, is a mystery. But he did, driven by a kind of demonic energy, for which in the end he paid a heavy price.

The lease of the Devonshire Terrace house was up, and anyhow it was now too small for the growing Dickens family. So a considerably larger house was found in Tavistock Square. Known as Tavistock House, it was to be his last London address. It was in very bad condition, and months were spent cleaning, decorating and altering it, while the family passed the summer in Broadstairs again. His daughters Mamey and Katey were now fourteen and twelve respectively, old enough to have a room of their own and to report how their father, with his military passion for order and neatness, inspected this room every morning, like a conscientious commanding officer. Though kind and generous and 'inimitable' (his favourite adjective for himself) at parties and picnics, domestically Dickens was something of a martinet, demanding tidiness everywhere. His wife, poor woman, fitted badly into this strict pattern.

A contemporary cartoon of Dickens and his fellow-writers discussing the controversial issue of copyright

Her health was not good, after so much child-bearing, and over and above that, probably because she was unsure of herself and unhappy, she was what would be called now 'accident-prone'. Something unpleasant or ridiculous was always happening to her: at a dinner party her bracelets would drop into the soup, and at the seaside or in the country she was for ever having accidents, falling and bruising herself. Dickens would laugh at the bracelets or offer sympathy for the accidents, but her unusual clumsiness was by this time a source of permanent irritation to him, and more and more, when he wanted to enjoy himself, he left her behind. His favourite companion now, for a holiday tour or an evening's jaunt, was Wilkie Collins, a gentle sweet-tempered man but very much a Bohemian type, who liked disreputable night life and cared nothing for Victorian respectability. It was the unhappy rebel in Dickens, lurking behind the *persona* of the earnest-minded public man, who dictated this choice of a companion.

An early photograph of Bleak House at Broadstairs

Dickens was now writing *Bleak House*, and when he had nearly finished it, in the early summer of 1853, he felt tired and not at all well. He took the family across to France, where they spent the summer in an odd château just outside Boulogne. He finished the book at the end of a very stormy August, fitting weather for its final scenes of darkness and violence. There was no doubt about its popularity, for the monthly parts were selling ten thousand more than even those of *David Copperfield* had done. This does not surprise us now, when it is recognised as one of Dickens's most powerful novels, but those of his con-temporaries who disliked this later work, declaring it to be sadly inferior to his early novels, ought to have been astonished. *Bleak House* has its weaknesses. There is too much improbability, encouraging melodrama, in its complicated plot. There are too many important characters not sharply realised. The Esther Summerson narrative is a clumsy mistake. The caricatures of Landor and

An illustration from *Bleak House*

Leigh Hunt, as Boythorn and Skimpole, we could well do without. Nevertheless, *Bleak House* is a wonderfully integrated fiction, of great power. It succeeds
on several different levels of interest and meaning. It is, among other things, a
highly dramatic study of our modern interdependence. It is a grim satire of
the Law's delays, but it goes much deeper than that, for the Court of Chancery
in the suffocating fog is itself a symbol of our whole society in its life-denying
and loveless aspects. And all this was better understood, perhaps in an instinctive
fashion, by the mass of ordinary readers than it was by most of the reviewers
and critics, many of them giving the book unfavourable notices. But of course
the society he was now challenging was striking back at Dickens.

After Boulogne, he went on holiday to Italy with Wilkie Collins and Augustus Egg, and at Naples met Henry Layard, the archaeologist, who had just
become a Liberal M.P. Equally concerned about the condition of England,

A playbill for amateur theatricals at Tavistock House

both hot for reform, Dickens and Layard soon became friends and had many long talks. It is more than likely that *Hard Times*, which Dickens was now planning, was much influenced by these talks. He returned to England in good time for Christmas, and to keep a promise he had made to give public readings of his two Christmas Books, the *Carol* and *The Cricket on the Hearth*, at Birmingham Town Hall. These readings were so wildly successful, and Dickens was so delighted by the way in which he could almost mesmerise such large audiences, that the idea—the fatal idea as it turned out to be in the end—of giving a series of public readings must have come to him first in Birmingham.

Early the following year, 1854, having begun work on *Hard Times* and needing more background for the novel, he paid a visit to Preston, where a big strike was in progress. The town, which he detested, was actually very quiet, and two meetings of strikers did not offer him any drama, though they deepened his sympathy with the men. He was now very much the ardent reformer, and the appalling muddle of the Crimean War, following soon afterwards, only confirmed him in his opinion that the governing classes were hopelessly inept and the country itself in a desperate condition. Meanwhile, *Hard Times* was

A scene from a Dickens production: *The Frozen Deep*

proving to be a very hard task, at which he worked with more will-power than enthusiasm. Although as a serial in *Household Words* it was at once successful, doubling the circulation, *Hard Times* has never been much liked, except by a few Marxist or socialist critics, like Shaw, who see it as an attack upon an in-dustrial capitalist society. And this of course it is, a very savage attack. But we may agree with its social criticism and yet still find it unconvincing and un-attractive as a novel, which is, after all, what it declares itself to be. Cer-tainly the Coketown scene is very grim, but there is no reason why it should not be: industrial England in the 1850's *was* very grim. But though as a social critic Dickens is often sharp, witty, perceptive, here as a novelist he seems un-certain and uneasy. A character like Gradgrind should be either more of a rounded human being or even less of one, simply a figure in a morality play. Again, a character like Stephen Blackpool seems to demand a different kind of novel; it is as if a pencil drawing had found its way on to a poster. Considered strictly as fiction, not as polemics, *Hard Times* does not succeed; it fails to hold and to satisfy the imagination; and we find it difficult to believe that those few critics who admire it excessively are not forcing their admiration.

There were a few more Christmas readings, still for charity. And Wilkie Collins wrote a play about a lighthouse, especially for the Dickens troupe. The house at Gad's Hill was to be sold soon, Dickens learned, and he decided to make an offer for it. Then, after more than twenty years, Maria Beadnell, now Mrs Winter, wrote to him out of the blue. The fact that this letter excited him at once only shows how ready he was now for some sort of romance. His replies to her are eager, sentimental, intimate. His youth is alive in him again. But when they met he found the delicious heart-breaking little Maria now a fat foolish woman with an irritatingly affected manner, all arch looks, head-tossings, and giggles. She made all the youthful emotion he had been feeling seem as ridiculous as she was. It was a bitter disappointment, a grotesque anti-climax to all his day-dreaming. He had to laugh at himself, once he had re-covered from the first shock. A few months later, when Flora Finching arrived in *Little Dorrit*, he laughed at her too, tastelessly and rather cruelly in the circumstances, for after all it was he who had deceived the poor woman into believing he was still in love with her. It is not a pleasant episode and Dickens cuts a poor figure in it. But it meant an end to any secret sentimental dream of the long-lost bewitching Maria. It also meant that there was now a vacancy that sooner or later, with Dickens in this state of mind, would have to be filled.

Mrs Winter *née* Maria Beadnell

The Paris boulevards during the Second Empire

First, however, there was a happy interlude. He and Georgina went over to Paris and found a suitable apartment that had a fine view of the *Champs Elysées*. And there the family was moved. Dickens's work was now well known, and in Paris, unlike London, authors were personages of some importance. This was the Paris, gay, luxurious, glittering, of the Second Empire at its height. He had to spend a few days every month in London, to attend to *Household Words*, and now, comparing it with Paris, London seemed to him heavier, darker and drearier than ever. He began to feel he never wanted to live there again. After attending the international exhibition of art, held in Paris during the time he was there, he could not help criticising adversely the English painters, many of them friends of his: 'What we know is wanting in the men,' he wrote, 'is wanting in their works. . . . There is a horrid respectability about most of the best of them. . . .' And then again: 'Mere form and conventionalities usurp, in English art, as in English government and social relations, the place of living force and truth. . . .' All this accounts for both the savage satire and the curious grey melancholy that crept into the novel he was writing—*Little Dorrit*.

Newgate Gaol; it was outside this grim prison that public hangings took place, which Dickens violently opposed

Prisons of every sort had always fascinated Dickens, haunted by his boyhood memories of the Marshalsea. *Little Dorrit* is dominated by prisons, and before we have reached the end of it we realise that society itself is only another and larger prison. Most of its characters are serving sentences of one sort or another. Though the story, perhaps mistakenly, was set back in time, it belongs essentially to the 1850's when it was written. (It was published in volume form in 1857.) Much of its symbolism, together with the force of its Circumlocution Office satire, was missed by Dickens's contemporaries. Thackeray, who may have seen something of himself in the character of Henry Gowan, said it was 'damned stupid'. But Bernard Shaw, years later, declared it to be 'a more seditious book than *Das Kapital*'. It is the work of a man who is angry and half despairing but who has not yet abandoned all hope. With the exception of Little Dorrit herself, who is conceived and presented in the old Dickens style, its chief characters show a new subtlety of modelling; they are exhibited in the round, with both light and shade. (The original title was *Nobody's Fault*, and many of the chapter headings suggest this theme.) It is a novel that the earlier Dickens would not have known how to write, and is very much the work of his new but tormented maturity.

After finishing *Little Dorrit* and returning to London, Dickens was altogether too restless and unhappy to begin writing another book. He was in a state of mind that encourages unwise decisions and almost inevitably leads to catastrophic events. The remainder of his life was shaped and coloured by what happened now. He fell in love, and was as blindly infatuated as he had been in his youth, pursuing the elusive Maria Beadnell. He separated from his wife, the mother of his ten children, in circumstances that injured his reputation and cost him many good friendships. He made the fatal decision—fatal because it shortened his life—to give public readings on a professional basis. All his last years lay in the shadow of these events.

The woman he fell in love with was a pretty fair-haired young actress called Ellen Ternan. It is said that he first met her when she was about sixteen, and he discovered her weeping behind the scenes at the Haymarket because she felt her stage costume was too immodest. (If this is true, then she probably produced a few tears to arouse his interest, for she belonged to a theatrical family, knew what the stage demanded, and can hardly have been suddenly upset by a costume she had worn several times before.) What is certain is that Ellen, her

A scene from *Little Dorrit* in the Marshalsea

Ellen Ternan
with her two sisters

sister Maria, and their mother, all professional actresses, were engaged for a production of *The Frozen Deep* in Manchester. This was a melodrama about Arctic explorers written by Wilkie Collins, with some help from Dickens. It had already been done in London, with Dickens managing it, playing the chief role, and even growing a beard to look more like an Arctic explorer. But for the much larger theatre in Manchester, lady amateurs would not do, it was necessary to have experienced professional actresses. So the Ternan trio was engaged. Ellen's part was only a minor one. It was the tears of her sister Maria that fell on Dickens's moustache and beard as he played the dying explorer. But in the life that went on around the play, it was fair little Ellen, with her big blue eyes and pretty ways, who soon assumed the major role. That she should have made a fuss of him, that he should have flirted with her— there was nothing new in all this, for he had always been attracted by good-looking, high-spirited girls. But this time, his imagination laid a trap for him. He was fascinated; he became infatuated; he found himself in love. She was still in her teens, and he was nearing fifty.

Even now, when the secret is out after being closely guarded for more than half a century, we do not know very much about their relationship. We do know that some time after his separation from his wife, Ellen Ternan became his mistress; was installed in a house at Peckham, where she bore him a child who died.* (After Dickens's death, she married an invalidish schoolmaster called Robinson, had a son and a daughter, and lived until 1914. The fact that she left no record of her association with Dickens—to our great loss—is significant.) But on the basis of the available evidence, including the petulant wilful behaviour of his last heroines, obviously modelled on her, it is not unreasonable to assume that while she could not resist this passionate dominating famous man, she was not really in love with him. She confessed afterwards that the situation in which she found herself during these years was one she deeply disliked, and she probably helped to keep the secret not so much out of concern

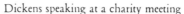
Dickens speaking at a charity meeting

* In his *Dickens Incognito* Mr Felix Aylmer suggests that Dickens and Ellen had a child who lived at least into early manhood. His opinion of Ellen herself is more favourable than mine.

Dickens with his family and friends in 1857

for Dickens's public reputation as out of a feeling of shame, and with it a desire to forget this chapter of her life. There does not seem to have been anything particularly unusual and striking about her as a young woman. But it so happened that this man of genius projected on to her the image of his heart's desire.

Obviously she could not go everywhere with him but she did travel with him at times, and his greatest worry, on his second visit to America, was whether he could take the chance of asking her to join him there. Georgina and the two daughters at Gad's Hill, and all his closer friends, knew about Ellen of course. But the association, lasting over ten years, was an astonishingly well-kept secret. Perhaps the old 'something wanting' no longer troubled him now that he had Ellen, but in every other respect she must have made life more difficult for him. We may safely guess that she resented her ambiguous position and all the secrecy surrounding it, and that she must have often expressed her dissatisfaction and have been demanding and hard to please. He was in his fifties and aging rapidly when she was still in her early twenties. They had little

　　　　　　　　　　　Old Drury Lane in Dickens's time ▶

Catherine Dickens
at the time of her separation
from Dickens

common ground of experience. They cannot have enjoyed very much of that cosy domesticity which Dickens not only celebrated in his novels but genuinely enjoyed himself for its own sake. Sometimes he must have felt guilty, at other times, what is perhaps even worse, he must have felt foolish. And then there was always the stifling necessity to keep it all a close secret. Any ease of body and mind that she brought him had to be paid for in anxiety and strain, and the price must have been heavy.

We are told that Dickens had been unhappy in his marriage for some years, but there can be no doubt that it was really his excited feelings about Ellen Ternan, some time before she became his mistress, that made him put an end to his marriage. A settlement was drawn up for an official separation. Kate was to live in London with her eldest son, Charley, while all the younger children remained at Gad's Hill with their father and their Aunt Georgina, who defied scandal by staying in the house that her sister had been compelled to quit. Though it may have been true that Georgina was closer to the children than

Kate was, that she had been running the household for years, this banishment of bewildered tearful Kate was not well done. We cannot help feeling that Dickens should either have left her long before they had had ten children or have seen his marriage through to the end. But now, wildly in love, seeing himself as a young man again and not a middle-aged husband and father, Dickens was incapable of sober judgment. He soon made matters worse.

Sweeping aside the protests of Forster and other alarmed friends, he drafted a solemn and fatuous statement about his domestic affairs, which at first he proposed to send to *The Times*. He did send it to *Punch*, and when his old friend, Mark Lemon, sensibly refused to print it, immediately quarrelled with him. His own publishers, Bradbury and Evans, were also the proprietors of *Punch*, so he quarrelled with them too. He insisted upon printing the statement in *Household Words*, and then, shortly afterwards, stopped publication of the magazine and started one in which Bradbury and Evans had no share—*All the Year Round*. He also arranged that his future novels should be published once

A 'thieves' den' in mid-Victorian London

Hablòt K. Browne (*Phiz*) in later life

more by Chapman and Hall. And any friends who took poor Kate's part, or even objected to his publishing his public statement, soon found themselves far out of favour. He behaved in fact far more like an infatuated youth than a mature man.

In one quarrel, however, he seems to have been on the right side. It had nothing to do with his private life. Edmund Yates, a young gossipy journalist, the son of a well-known actress, wrote an impertinent hostile account of Thackeray. Both Yates and Thackeray were members of the Garrick Club. Thackeray maintained that Yates's account of his style of talk could only be based on what Yates had overheard at the Club, and took his complaint to the Committee. Yates appealed to Dickens, also a member of the Garrick, and Dickens instantly agreed that Thackeray's official complaint was unjustified,

Edmund Yates

the Club not having been mentioned in the article. Nevertheless, Yates was told by the Committee that he must resign from the Club. Still backed by Dickens, he would not accept this decision, and for some months there was talk of a legal action, in which a notorious advocate would be employed. Nothing came of this, but during all these months literary and journalistic London was divided into two belligerent factions. Any friendship there had been between Dickens and Thackeray—and at no time had it been close and warm—was now destroyed. The quarrel only encouraged the legend, which survived both men, that there existed between them a bitter rivalry as competing novelists. This in fact was entirely untrue. Neither could fully appreciate the other's work simply because of their widely different temperaments, outlook, methods in fiction. In this particular quarrel, Dickens, supporting Yates, would seem to

A caricature of Thackeray and Dickens
at the time of their quarrel

have been in the right, for Thackeray, no matter how annoyed he might have been by Yates's slapdash attack on him (and in his early *Punch* days, Thackeray himself had been at least equally vindictive and unscrupulous), should not have taken his resentment to the Committee of the Garrick. Most journalists, especially those known as 'the Bohemians', supported Yates and Dickens, but the gentlemanly interests and what might be called Mandarin literary opinion were on Thackeray's side. And probably this injured Dickens's reputation in such circles.

We must now consider his decision to give professional public readings. Forster, still his chief adviser, was against them, holding them to be undignified for an author of his reputation. Dickens's excuse was that the readings would enable him to earn a good deal of money very quickly. He certainly needed the money for now he had three establishments to keep going—his

Ellen Ternan

own at Gad's Hill, Kate's in London, Ellen Ternan's at Peckham. But the profit they brought him was not the real reason why he insisted upon giving these readings. He needed the excitement of travel and triumphant personal appearances. He wanted to exercise magnetic power over great audiences he could see and hear, to listen to the laughter, the sobs, the applause, to satisfy himself directly and without doubt that to most people he was still 'the inimitable'. These were not really readings at all but carefully rehearsed and staged performances, for which the original texts were cut and altered in various other ways, to produce an immediate dramatic effect.

The characters in all their variety were brilliantly acted. It was in fact a stupendous one-man theatrical production. All accounts agree that in humour, pathos, or sheer terror, he was unmatched, appearing almost to hypnotise his enormous audiences.

Dickens at work at Gad's Hill Place

The 'committee of concoction', a cartoon satirising Dickens at work with his friends

These performances, however, were like a drug, of which he had to have increasingly stronger doses. Before he had done with them, he was terrifying his audiences with the murder of Nancy by Sykes, tearing himself to pieces each night. Moreover, although he tried to save his energy for his appearances at the reading desk—he carried it round with him, for it was specially constructed and brilliantly lit with gas lamps—he could not escape from his enthusiastic admirers everywhere, was rarely left alone for long, so that the nervous wear-and-tear of these tours and the drain on his energy were appalling. He had always been capable of great exertion, tiring out his companions, but constitutionally he was not really strong. He aged fast during these years, and many of the people who saw him were shocked to discover how old he looked. Again and again he was warned that he must stop these readings and work quietly in his study. But he persisted, not because of the money, not entirely because of the excitement and applause, but out of a kind of strange despair,

The Frontispiece from
A Tale of Two Cities

as if he felt doomed to move towards disaster. The most famous novelist in the world—for that is what he was during these 1860's—had decided, on the deepest level of his personality, to wear himself out.

Something of this, together with a feeling for rebellion in its most violent form, finds its way into *A Tale of Two Cities*. Much influenced by Carlyle's *French Revolution*, which Dickens greatly admired, this romantic tale, which has little humour and no crowded gallery of characters, has nothing in common with the novels of his maturity, or indeed with his fiction in general. Its sharp action and complicated plotting, not afraid of astonishing coincidences, give it a theatrical air. A sentimental melodrama based on this tale and called *The Only Way* was still popular for many years of our own century. Perhaps the noble

Dickens reading to his daughters at Gad's Hill

Ellen Ternan's mother as she appeared on the stage in *All's Well That Ends Well*

renunciation of Sydney Carton, a character into which some of Dickens's self-pity finds its way, is best enjoyed against a painted backcloth and with incidental music.

His next novel, *Great Expectations*, had to be written first as a weekly serial for *All The Year Round*, because a story by Charles Lever that was being serialised was not popular and circulation was falling. It was a difficult time for Dickens. He saw Ellen Ternan constantly but she was still living with her mother. His boys were growing up and he had to decide what they ought to do. One of his brothers died, and so did several of his old friends. But he seemed to have a desire to have done with the past. At Gad's Hill he made a great bonfire of the

The chalet where Dickens
used to work at Gad's Hill

Dickens with family
and friends at Gad's Hill

Georgina Hogarth
'the best and truest
friend man ever had'

letters and private papers of the last twenty years, hundreds of letters, from Carlyle, Tennyson, Browning, Rogers, Sydney Smith, Bulwer-Lytton, Lady Blessington, Ainsworth, Captain Marryat, Cruikshank and Maclise and other artists, all vanishing into the flames.

But some of his own distant past, the shame of the blacking warehouse episode, crept into *Great Expectations*. Not that it was autobiographical even in the limited sense that *David Copperfield* was, in spite of the fact that Pip tells his own story. But that past and what Dickens now felt had been his wrong attitude towards it are there in the story. Possibly some of his present too, for it is easy to believe that certain less agreeable aspects of Ellen may have suggested Estella. And Dickens earlier could not have created the relationship, so bitter and unrewarding, between Pip and Estella. It is a pity that when the first proofs of the novel came to hand, he was staying with Bulwer-Lytton at Knebworth and

FROM WHOM WE HAVE
GREAT EXPECTATIONS

A cartoon which appeared in London after the publication of *Great Expectations*

Dickens about to
give a reading
in public

agreed, at his host's urgent request, to soften the original ending. Apart from this final false note, *Great Expectations* deserves to be, as it always has been, one of his most popular novels. It has not the panoramic sweep and the intricate symbolism of the other later novels, but it has a sharper narrative, more cunningly blended humour, a wonderful study of a hopeless infatuation, and its social criticism of the power of wealth and the Victorian notion of an idle 'gentleman of means' is solidly embedded in Pip's account of himself.

After he had finished with *Great Expectations*, which was published in three volumes when it had ended its serial run, Dickens set out in the late autumn of

Arthur Smith, the first manager for Dickens's tours

John Leech, the great
'Punch' caricaturist

1861 to give no fewer than fifty public readings. But his extremely efficient
manager, Arthur Smith, had died, and this tour was sadly mismanaged—
it was also interrupted by the death of the Prince Consort—so that, although in
the end it was a triumphant success, it had made increased demands on his
nervous energy and stamina. For the following two years, until *Our Mutual
Friend* began to be issued in monthly parts in the spring of 1864, he did little
writing. Though now settled at Gad's Hill he spent much time in London,
and when Georgina was convalescent after a serious illness, he rented a house
in Paris for her and himself and his daughter Mary. It was a time when death
struck hard: his mother, Kate's mother, Augustus Egg, Thackeray, John
Leech, and the son, Walter Landor Dickens, whom he had shipped out to
India, where the boy died on the last day of 1863. After too much dining out
in London, Dickens began to suffer from sharp pains in his left leg and foot,
which had to have frequent fomentations. This trouble, together with hard work
on *Our Mutual Friend*, kept him for some time in comparative quiet at Gad's
Hill. But then he took Ellen Ternan to France, and on their return to England

the train from Folkestone jumped a gap in the line that was being repaired. It was a very bad accident, eight coaches crashing down a river bank, many passengers being killed and injured. Neither Dickens nor Ellen was hurt, and Dickens behaved with fine courage and coolness, doing what he could to assist the dying and injured. The real shock came afterwards, and for months he felt shaky and very nervous about railway journeys. Perhaps he never really recovered from it.

After the shilling monthly parts, *Our Mutual Friend* was published in two volumes late in 1865. It was his last completed novel, and is unquestionably one of his best. Here there is no going back in time. This is the booming, rapidly expanding London of the 1860's, full of new futile people like the Veneerings. It is a city of get-rich-quicks. It is also a city in which ordure, garbage and rubbish are carted away and dumped, gradually forming huge

The Staplehurst railway disaster

London dust-heaps near King's Cross

piles generally known as 'dust-heaps'. (These were valuable: one of them was sold for £40,000.) Dickens knew all about them, because years before he wrote *Our Mutual Friend* he had printed an article in *Household Words* dealing with rich dust-contractors, the masters of the heaps. It was a stroke of genius to base his story on the wealth created by these mountains of muck. London itself of course is only another dust-heap. *Our Mutual Friend* is a dark mixture of anger and despair. As a novel it has its faults. It is too dusty, joyless; its plot is too complicated and really belongs to another kind of novel; its broad non-satirical humour, as distinct from its satire which is wonderful, is forced, mechanical; and the author too often calls his readers to attention and addresses them from a platform. But the chief characters, especially Eugene Wrayburn, Bradley Headstone and Bella Wilfer, are marvellously well done; and the satirical sketches of Podsnap and his circle are superb. Its elaborate symbolism, reducing a whole society and all its values to garbage and dust, is an astonishingly sustained effort of Dickens's creative imagination. It is angry satire charged with poetic force.

Though he was obviously in poor health throughout 1866, he accepted an offer from Messrs. Chappell to give thirty readings, over a wide area, at £50 a night with all his expenses paid. Fortunately for Dickens they found a good man, George Dolby, to manage the tour. It was Dolby who went to America to make all the arrangements for Dickens to give a series of readings over there.

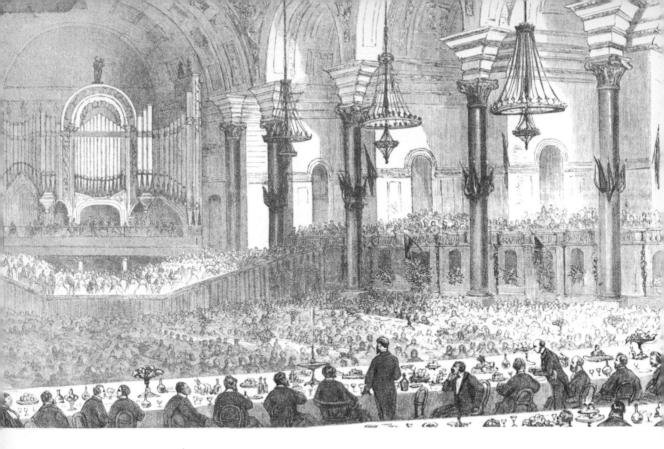

A grand banquet given in Dickens's honour

Dickens had been considering an American tour some years before, but then came the Civil War. (Oddly enough, in view of his earlier attacks on slavery, his sympathies were with the South.) Now the War was over, and J. T. Fields and a group of friends in Boston offered Dickens a guarantee of £10,000 that he could bank in London before he sailed. Forster and other friends were all against this American tour, but when Dolby reported an immense eagerness to hear him, he agreed to go. A series of farewell dinners concluded with a tremendous public banquet at the Freemasons' Hall, where there were over four hundred male guests, a hundred ladies waving handkerchiefs from one gallery, and in another the full brass of the band of the Grenadier Guards. Dickens sailed from Liverpool in November 1867, and did not return home until the following May.

This second American visit was quite different from the first, twenty-five years before. He never went as far as the Middle West this time. He gave most of his readings in Boston and New York, though he did go again to Baltimore

'Farewell to Dickens', John Bull sends Dickens off on his trip to America

and Washington and also performed in a number of smaller Eastern towns. There were no more attacks in the newspapers, only some grumbling about the way in which Dolby was handling his ticket problems. The demand for tickets everywhere was enormous, the whole tour being a wonderful success. But Dickens's condition was now worse than ever, and only by resting whenever he could, eating little solid food, exerting his astonishing power of will, was he able to go through with it. During the last days in New York, when he had not only to read but also to speak at a sumptuous press banquet, he was in constant severe pain, given medical attention every day, and often collapsed as soon as he was out of the public view. Before sailing, he paid a handsome tribute to the warmth and generosity of his American hosts and to all the many changes for the better he had noticed during this visit. Although the dollar had still not recovered from the War, the rate of exchange being about seven to the pound, he had earned about £20,000. But it had been done the hard way, probably shortening his life.

THE BRITISH LION IN AMERICA (Charles Dickens)

'The British Lion
in America',
an American cartoon

The voyage rested and refreshed him. Even his doctor said he looked much better than when he set out for America. There was much to do. His assistant editor, Willis, had had an accident, so Dickens had to look after *All the Year Round* and also write some short pieces for it. Gad's Hill saw plenty of visitors. The youngest son, Plorn, was shipped off to Australia, to join his older brother there. Then, in the late autumn, Dickens was faced with the contract he had made with Messrs. Chappell, to give a hundred readings, for which he would be paid £8,000. Now he decided, against all advice, to bring into his programme, after careful rehearsal of all its horrible effects, the murder scene from

Dickens's readings
as seen by one
American newspaper

Oliver Twist, a scene that terrified his audiences and nearly always left him prostrated. Why did he insist upon doing it? It was as if something dark and murderous in him had to find an outlet.

But then why did he persist in going on with the readings, now that he could no longer pretend he was not a sick man, threatened with paralysis all down his left side, compelled to have medical attention in one town after another? Certainly he needed money, with so many people dependent upon him, but he was in no desperate need of it and could earn a handsome living writing quietly at home. What made him defy his doctors and override the

The Press dinner given to Dickens in New York in 1868

protests of his family and friends? It must have been nothing short of a suicidal despair. This famous Dickens, who had waved to the New York crowds like a departing sovereign, who had arrived home through Kentish villages bright with flags of welcome, who appeared to have everything he could have dreamt of as a young man, did not care at heart whether he lived or died. His inner world was turning to dust, ashes and darkness. It is true that he detested the society of his time and knew now he could never feel at home in it. It is true that his personal and family life had disappointed him. (Ellen Ternan too, probably, for it is significant that although he named her in his will, she was left only £1,000.) It is equally true—and this is something that critics and readers too often forget—that his prodigious creative efforts had made appalling demands on his nervous energy. (Shakespeare died, an old man, at fifty-two.) But though so much, and more, is true, the fundamental reason why he followed such a suicidal course lies deep in his inner world, where a boy who had never grown up was still wondering if he would ever escape from the blacking warehouse.

New York again. Broadway in the 1860's

A photograph of Dickens taken during his American tour

It is in these murky depths that *The Mystery of Edwin Drood* must have been conceived—the story that he began to work at, slowly, laboriously, and that he never lived to complete, leaving it one of literature's most famous riddles. Possibly he saw himself attempting the kind of involved mystery tale that his friend Wilkie Collins had done so successfully, but giving it a richer atmosphere and more depth as well as some oriental and occult additions—opium, thuggery, hypnotism, split personality. But whether he knew it or not, he was dredging his own depths. He was a divided man, for whom murder had always had a fascination, telling the story of another divided man who committed a murder. The scene is Cloisterham, really his old favourite, Rochester, good Dickens country; but the atmosphere is very different, there are sinister signs everywhere, marks of death, hints of mystery, the very sun might be shining in an opium dream. Only six of its monthly parts were written and published, coming out from April to September 1870, but we have enough of the strange mysterious tale to make us realise that Jasper is the central key figure, and to guess that this man from the East is both a murderer and a bewildered innocent, divided between extreme evil and goodness, and that this elaborate tale is also a parable

Charles Fechter, a friend of Dickens, in his play *No Thoroughfare*

...nlas are surpassing the anthem, when the busy old gleaner in the air, and the rich trees washing in the balmy air. Changes of ... songs of ... seem to pour yonder woods and fields — or rather from the one great yonder where all the cultivated ... its building time — penetrate into the Cathedral. ... its colours, and ... the Resurrection and the Life. The cold stone tombs of centuries grow warm, and flecks of brightness dart into the sternest marble corners of the building, fluttering everywhere like ... things.

... the old ... care in distance, ... and on locks and ... Mrs Tope and ... come ... peeping down from the ... ... in the left ... from stops of pedals, come roaring from various quarters built to the great ... as is presumed to ... in ... situation, and to those that tell and organ are ... small and straggling ... congregation: chiefly from Minor Canon Corner and the ... care at Crisparkle, fresh and bright, and his ministering between ... ... so fresh and bright, come the choir in a hurry (always in a hurry), and ... like children sinking to ... and comes Mr Jasper ... choir collection ... Last of all comes ... Royal Highness the Princess Puffer.

The service is well advanced before Mr Datchery can discern the Royal ... self withdrawn from the choir-master's view, in regard to him with the closest ... and so — yes. Mr Datchery sees her doing it. Shakes her fist at him, which the pillar shelter.

Mr Datchery looks again to convince himself ... on the under brackets of the stall seats, as ... as the big hag ... the sacred books — for his wips (and according to the shakes her fist at the leader of the choir ... and ... the greatest actor of the choir, having eluded the vigilance of Tope by shifting ... in which he is an adept. Deputy peeps through the ... and stares astounded from the threatener to the threatened

The service comes to an end, and the services disperse to fast. Mr Datchery accosts his last new acquaintance outside, when the choir ... their bedgowns off, as they are but now ... ... "Well! and have I seen him."
"I've seen him dearly; I've seen him."
"And you know him?"
"Know him! Better far, than all the Reverend Parsons put than them him."

Mrs Tope's care has spread a very neat clean breakfast for her lodger. He sitting down to ... he opens his corner cupboard door; takes his bit of chalk on its face; adds one thick line to the score, extending from the top ... ... to the bottom; and then falls to with an appetite.

Dickens crosses
the Channel;
a French cartoon in 1868

and perhaps, consciously or unconsciously for Dickens, a chapter of profound self-revelation, a kind of confession. Shaw, wanting more social criticism, could only see in this last work 'a gesture by a man already three-quarters dead', but this is insensitive criticism, for Dickens never worked better to create the atmosphere he wanted, to suggest subtle undertones and overtones, than he did in these early chapters of *Edwin Drood*. It is as if, three-quarters dead though he might be, he was feeling his way towards yet another sort of fiction.

Somehow or other, in March 1870, he got through his final reading, to a great cheering audience in St James's Hall. 'From these garish lights,' he said

◀ The last page that Dickens ever wrote, from *Edwin Drood*

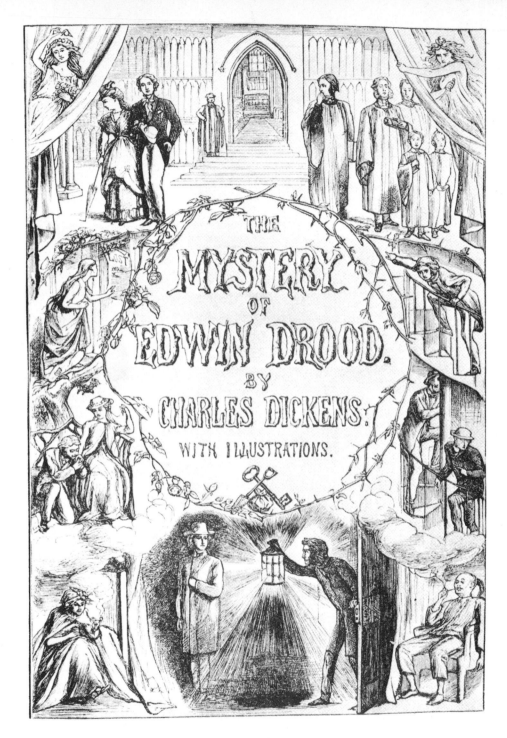

The cover in which the instalments of *Edwin Drood* appeared

Dickens's last reading in 1870

at the end, his face wet with tears, 'I vanish now for evermore with a heartfelt, grateful, respectful and affectionate farewell.' During these weeks in London, perhaps chiefly to please his unmarried daughter Mary who was with him there, he dragged himself into the great houses of the Establishment. He was presented to the Prince of Wales at a levée; Mary was presented to the Queen; both of them were invited to a Court Ball; he breakfasted with Gladstone; he replied to the toast of Literature at the Academy Dinner; and he had a long audience with Queen Victoria, who kept him standing for an hour and a half. It was generally believed, and has been repeated by some of his biographers, that he was offered a baronetcy and accepted it; but in his excellent two-volume biography, the best we have had so far, Mr Edgar Johnson suggests that this rumour originated in a facetious letter Dickens wrote to Helps, the Clerk of the Privy Council. What is certain is that up to the end of May, barely able to hobble around, he remained in London, dining and going to the theatre with the great, and even managing some private theatricals. But there are hints that he knew his time was running out.

Early in June he went to Gad's Hill, to work on *Edwin Drood* every morning in the little Swiss chalet in the garden. His daughter Katey came down for the week-end, and on Sunday she sat up late with her father, who told her that he wished he had been 'a better father, and a better man'. He also spoke of his hopes for *Edwin Drood*—'if, please God, I live to finish it'. After Katey returned to London, her sister Mary left Gad's Hill to join her there. On June 8 Dickens for once worked all day and even wrote a few letters in his study before dinner. In the dining-room Georgina saw that he was suffering from some pain, and he told her that for an hour he had been very ill. Suddenly he pushed himself up from the table, saying he must go to London at once. Then he collapsed, and Georgina and the servants had to lift him on to the sofa. There he stayed, unconscious, all night. He had had a severe paralytic stroke, affecting the brain. He never recovered consciousness, and just after six, the following afternoon, he died. He was fifty-eight.

The news of his death shocked and saddened the whole world. It was as if a great light had gone out. But, even now, irony had not done with him. He had wanted the quietest of funerals and had hoped to be buried in a little local grave-yard; he had cared nothing for the historic past and tradition; he had always been at odds with the English Establishment; but now *The Times*, which had disliked so much of what he had written, declared that he must be buried in Westminster Abbey. His grave there was left open for several days, and thousands and thousands of people filed past it. Indeed, for months afterwards fresh flowers were heaped around his tombstone. England had much to mourn, for now she had lost the most prodigal creative genius her literature had known since Shakespeare. But we have only to open one of the books bearing his name, books that have been reprinted so many times during the last ninety years, to discover that Charles Dickens is still alive.

The crowd paying their last respects to Dickens at Westminster Abbey ▶

'The Empty Chair': Gad's Hill Place on June 9, 1870

1812 February 7. Charles Dickens is born at 387 Mile End Terrace, Portsmouth.

1817 The Dickens family moves to Chatham, where Dickens spends his first schooldays.

1822–24 Dickens's father is recalled to London. The family moves from Chatham into a poor part of Camden Town. Their rapidly worsening financial situation results in John Dickens's arrest for debt. His family lodge with him for a while. Charles is sent to work in Warren's Blacking Warehouse, where he spends about six months.

1824–26 Dickens goes back to school at the Wellington House Academy.

1827–28 Dickens works as a clerk in an attorney's office. In the evenings he studies shorthand.

1829 He meets Maria Beadnell, the daughter of a London banker, and falls in love with her.

1829–31 Dickens gains employment as a shorthand-writer for the Proctors in Doctors' Commons. In his spare time he reads at the British Museum.

1832–33 He begins his career as a journalist, doing general reporting for the *True Sun* and Parliamentary reporting for *The Mirror of Parliament.*

1833 December: Dickens's first published work appears in the *Monthly Magazine.*

1834 August: He is taken on as a full-time Parliamentary reporter by the *Morning Chronicle*, and uses the pen-name 'Boz' for the first time.

1835 Dickens makes his name as a Parliamentary reporter and political correspondent. He covers events all over the country. He becomes friendly with William Harrison Ainsworth who introduces him to Macrone, his first publisher.

1836 February: Publication of *Sketches by Boz*.
April: *The Pickwick Papers* published in serial form—a great success.
Dickens leaves the *Morning Chronicle* in order to devote himself to his writing.
April: Dickens marries Catherine Hogarth.

1837 May: Death of Mary Hogarth, Dickens's sister-in-law.

1838 Dickens repeats his success with the publication of *Oliver Twist*.

1839 Publication of *Nicholas Nickleby*. Dickens's reputation grows: he makes many new friends and is introduced into fashionable London literary society.

1840–41 Dickens creates *Master Humphrey's Clock*, a weekly periodical in which *The Old Curiosity Shop* and *Barnaby Rudge* are first published.

1842 January–June: Dickens visits the United States. He receives a great welcome, but is disillusioned by the country.
October: Publication of *American Notes* which causes a furore in America.

1843–44 Publication of *Martin Chuzzlewitt* and *A Christmas Carol*. Dickens and his family go abroad, and settle in Genoa.

1844 December: Dickens returns to London to read *The Chimes* to his friends, then goes back to the Continent.

1845 Dickens and his family make a tour through Italy and France, before returning to England. Dickens and Forster act in Jonson's *Every Man in his Humour* for charity.

1846 January: First publication of the *Daily News* under Dickens's editorship. Resigns after three weeks and goes abroad again. He lives with his family in Lausanne and Paris, where he meets French literary celebrities.

1846–50 Dickens writes *Dombey and Son* and *Christmas Stories*, is immersed in social, philanthropic and journalistic activities, produces and acts in amateur theatricals.

1849 May: Publication of first instalment of *David Copperfield*, Dickens's favourite and probably most successful novel.

1850 March: Dickens begins publication of *Household Words*.

1851 May: Dickens and his amateur company perform before the Queen and the Prince Consort at Devonshire House, London.
Dickens moves to Tavistock House in Bloomsbury.

1852 Publication of *Bleak House* begins.

1853 Dickens spends the summer at Boulogne where he writes the last numbers of *Bleak House*.
In October he sets off on another tour of Italy with Wilkie Collins and Augustus Egg.

1854 Publication of *Hard Times*. Dickens spends another summer at Boulogne.

1855 February: Dickens meets Maria Beadnell —now Mrs. Winter—again.
November: Dickens goes to Paris where he spends the next six months.
December: Publication begins of *Little Dorrit*.

1856 Dickens mingles with the Paris literary and artistic society again.
March: Dickens buys Gad's Hill Place, which is to be his last permanent home.
June: He settles at Boulogne again for the summer.

1857 January: Performance of Wilkie Collins's play *The Frozen Deep* at Tavistock House.
June 30: Dickens gives his first public reading at St. Martin's Hall, London.

1858 Dickens falls in love with Ellen Ternan and is separated from his wife; he makes a personal statement about his private life on the front page of *Household Words* for June 10.
He quarrels with Thackeray over the 'Yates' affair.

1859 Publication of *A Tale of Two Cities*. Dickens begins a new periodical *All the Year Round*.

1859–70 During this period Dickens travels all over England giving public readings of his works.

1860–61 Publication of *Great Expectations*.

1864–65 Publication of *Our Mutual Friend*.

1865 June: Dickens is involved in the Staplehurst railway accident. From this time his health begins to deteriorate rapidly.

1867–68 Dickens's second visit to the United States where he gives public readings—a huge success. He is feted by the Press Club in New York.

1868 May: Dickens returns to England.

1869 Dickens gives further readings in England, attends many public functions.

1870 March: Dickens gives his last public reading in London, and is received in audience by Queen Victoria.
April: Publication of the first instalment of *The Mystery of Edwin Drood*, and last public appearance of Dickens at a Royal Academy Dinner.
June 8: Dickens collapses from a stroke at Gad's Hill Place and dies the following day.
June 14: Dickens's remains are buried in the Poet's Corner at Westminster Abbey.

Frontispiece. This striking photograph was taken by Mayall, a master of the 'daguerrotype' technique, in 1849, when Dickens was reaching the full maturity of his powers as a writer. One year later *David Copperfield* was published. *Radio Times Hulton Picture Library.*

Page

5 ALTHOUGH DICKENS WAS BORN NEAR PORTSMOUTH, the family moved to Chatham early in 1816, where his father was employed at the Navy Pay Office in the Dockyard. *Thames and Hudson Archives.*

6 ELIZABETH DICKENS (1789–1863), a portrait by John W. Gilbert. Charles's mother was the daughter of Charles Barrow, an important official at Somerset House who was later involved in a financial scandal. She met John Dickens through her brother who was his friend and colleague. *The Dickens Fellowship.*

JOHN DICKENS (1785/6–1851) was immortalised as 'Mr. Micawber' in *David Copperfield*. Although a kind father to his children, he was hopelessly improvident and Charles's childhood miseries were mainly due to his father's continual financial crises. *Specially photographed from an engraving.*

7 THE LITTLE HOUSE in which the Dickens family lived at Chatham from 1817 to 1821. Later, due to John Dickens's financial difficulties, they had to move to a poorer quarter of the town. *The Dickens Fellowship.*

THIS PHOTOGRAPH TAKEN AT THE TURN OF THE CENTURY shows Rochester High Street much as it was when Dickens was a boy and used to watch the coaches arriving from London. *The Dickens Fellowship.*

8–9 IT WAS IN THE COUNTRYSIDE AROUND CHATHAM and the neighbouring city of Rochester that Dickens spent some of the happiest days of his childhood. For the rest of his life Dickens cherished a special affection for this part of Kent. *Thames and Hudson Archives.*

9 YOUNG DICKENS must often have seen the passengers dismounting from the London coach in one of the great coaching-inns at Rochester. From Pierce Egan's *Life in London,* 1821. *Guildhall Library, London.*

10 AN EARLY PHOTOGRAPH of the house at no. 16 Bayham Street, Camden Town, where the Dickens family lived during the financial crisis of 1823–24 which culminated with John Dickens's arrest for debt. *The Dickens Fellowship.*

11 FOR SIX MONTHS YOUNG CHARLES DICKENS was employed sticking labels on pots of blacking at Warren's Blacking Warehouse. 'No words can express the secret agony of my soul', he was to write years afterwards. 'That I suffered in secret, and that I suffered exquisitely, no one ever knew but I.' *From a drawing by Fred Barnard.*

12 OLD HUNGERFORD STAIRS, LONDON. The blacking warehouse was a tumble-down old building near the water's edge below Charing Cross. The buildings were later destroyed to make room for a market. *The Dickens Fellowship.*

13 THE MARSHALSEA IN SOUTHWARK was a prison for debtors. Their families were allowed to visit them, and even share their lodgings in the prison. *Radio Times Hulton Picture Library.*

14 AFTER JOHN DICKENS HAD BEEN RE-LEASED from the Marshalsea, Charles Dickens spent the next two and a half years finishing his schooling at the Wellington House Academy, where he was known more for his lively high spirits than any great scholastic attainments. *The Dickens Fellowship.*

15 A SPECIMEN PAGE OF DICKENS'S NOTES IN SHORTHAND. Determined to become a newspaper reporter, Dickens set himself to study shorthand in the evenings, when he was working in a solicitor's office. He eventually became one of the fastest short-hand-writers in the country. *The Dickens Fellowship.*

16 DOCTORS' COMMONS: an archaic medley of various civil and ecclesiastical courts dealing mainly with wills and diocesan matters, until they were superseded in 1857 by the Probate Court. It was in these courts that Dickens spent the first two years of his career as a shorthand-writer. *The Dickens Fellowship.*

17 THE THEATRE was to be one of Dickens's life-long loves. While working as a short-hand reporter he decided to try his luck on the stage and applied to the stage manager at the Theatre Royal, Covent Garden, but fell ill on the day he was to have had an audition. *Radio Times Hulton Picture Library.*

18 THE EARLIEST KNOWN PORTRAIT OF DICKENS. Engraving from a miniature pain-ted in 1830 by his aunt, Mrs Janet Barrow. *The Dickens Fellowship.*

19 A CONTEMPORARY CARICATURE of one of the many, semi-amateur, unlicensed theatres that flourished in early nineteenth-century London, that Dickens used to visit. They specialised in sensational melodrama and broad farce, and generally charged a penny admission fee, which gave them their name. From James Grant's *Sketches in London*, 1838. *Radio Times Hulton Picture Library.*

20 GEORGE HOGARTH (1783–1870) was a fellow-reporter of Dickens's on the *Morning Chronicle*, and later editor of the *Evening Chronicle*. They became good friends and it was at Hogarth's house that Dickens met his daughter, Catherine, in 1835. *The Dickens Fellowship.*

21 A CONTEMPORARY PRINT of the Old Read-ing Room at the British Museum. In his early years as a reporter Dickens spent much of his spare time reading to make up for his interrupted education. *Collection R. A. Rudorff.*

22 AMATEUR THEATRICALS played a large part in Dickens's life. As early as 1833 he was producing and acting in plays with the aid of members of his family and friends, even having playbills printed like the one reproduced. *The Dickens Fellowship.*

'With fear and trembling' one November evening in 1833 Dickens placed his first literary composition 'into a dark letter-box in a dark office up a dark court in Fleet Street'. The office was that of the *Monthly Magazine* which printed Dickens's piece in its following issue. *The Dickens Fellowship.*

23 LONDON BRIDGE, thronged with omnibuses and pedestrians as Dickens must have seen it. From Gustave Doré's *London*, 1872. *Specially photographed.*

24 WILLIAM HARRISON AINSWORTH (1805–82) was the flamboyant and successful author of *Rookwood* and the *Tower of London*, sen-sational 'historical' novels. He first met Dickens in 1834 and shortly afterwards

introduced him to his first publisher, John Macrone. *Radio Times Hulton Picture Library.*

25 A TITLE PAGE from one of the volumes of *Sketches by Boz*, which first appeared in bound form in February 1836. It was a great success and received many favourable reviews. The illustrations were engraved by George Cruikshank (1792–1878), the greatest illustrator and caricaturist of his day. *Specially photographed.*

26 AN ILLUSTRATION BY CRUIKSHANK from *Sketches by Boz* of a London pawnshop. *Specially photographed.*

27 A SKETCH OF DICKENS by George Cruikshank, made at the time of their collaboration on *Sketches by Boz* and *Oliver Twist*. *The Dickens Fellowship.*

28 THE FIRST ILLUSTRATION in the *Pickwick Papers*, from a plate engraved by Robert Seymour. After doing a few more illustrations for the book he quarrelled with Dickens and committed suicide in a fit of depression. *Specially photographed.*

29 ROBERT SEYMOUR was succeeded after a short interval by Hablôt K. Browne who became one of Dickens's closest friends and collaborators and his best-known illustrator, under the pseudonym of 'Phiz'. *Specially photographed.*

31 THIS FAMOUS PICTURE BY 'PHIZ' of the Eatanswill by-election episode in the *Pickwick Papers* is an example of how politics appeared to Dickens, who had attended political meetings and elections all over the country while working as a reporter. *Specially photographed.*

32 *Bentley's Miscellany* was the magazine in which *Oliver Twist* first appeared in serial form. It was established by the London publisher, Richard Bentley, in 1836. He offered the editorship to Dickens who held it until his quarrel with Bentley in 1839. *The Dickens Fellowship.*

33 MARY HOGARTH, Dickens's sister-in-law, from a portrait by Hablôt K. Browne. Her early death probably inspired the character of Little Nell in *The Old Curiosity Shop*. *The Dickens Fellowship.*

MRS CHARLES DICKENS shortly after her marriage, from the portrait by Daniel Maclise, RA, who was a close friend of the family. *The Dickens Fellowship.*

34 TWO FAMOUS ILLUSTRATIONS from 'Oliver Twist' after the engravings by George Cruikshank. *Specially photographed.*

35 A PROFILE SKETCH by Maclise of Dickens, his wife, and Mary Hogarth, made shortly before Mary's death in 1837. *The Forster Collection. By courtesy of the Victoria and Albert Museum, London.*

36 ANGELA BURDETT COUTTS, later Baroness Burdett Coutts, was a philanthropic heiress who became Dickens's life-long friend and godmother to his first son. They collaborated in many charitable enterprises. *The Dickens Fellowship.*

37 SYDNEY SMITH (1771–1845), a clergyman who became Canon of St Paul's Cathedral, was a man of letters and a prominent member of the Holland House Whig 'set'. He was especially renowned for his wit and the charm of his manner. *Radio Times Hulton Picture Library.*

37 EDWARD BULWER-LYTTON (1803–73) was an MP and a writer of historical novels (*The*

Last Days of Pompeii, Rienzi). He was made baron in 1866. *Radio Times Hulton Picture Library.*

38 JOHN FORSTER (1812–76) was a journalist and man of letters. He became Dickens's closest friend and adviser. Although they often quarrelled their friendship lasted until Dickens's death. From a sketch made in May 1840 by Daniel Maclise. *The Dickens Fellowship.*

39 DICKENS IN 1839. This portrait, painted by Maclise in 1839, is known as the 'Nickleby Portrait' as an engraving after it was used as a frontispiece to *Nicholas Nickleby. By courtesy of the Trustees of the National Portrait Gallery, London.*

40 THOMAS CARLYLE (1795–1881), the famous political philosopher and historian, was later to inspire Dickens's *Tale of Two Cities* with his work on the French Revolution. From an early daguerrotype. *The Dickens Fellowship.*

CARLYLE'S WIFE JANE (1801–86) shared her husband's admiration for Dickens, whom they frequently visited. She was known as one of the finest, wittiest letter-writers of the age. *The Dickens Fellowship.*

41 DEVONSHIRE TERRACE, by Regent's Park, was Dickens's London residence from 1839 to 1851. After a sketch made by David Maclise. *The Dickens Fellowship.*

42 BROADSTAIRS. For many years this small seaside town was Dickens's favourite summer holiday resort. From an old print. *The Dickens Fellowship.*

43 'THE INTERNAL ECONOMY OF DOTHEBOYS HALL': an illustration by 'Phiz' from *Nicholas Nickleby*, 1839. *Specially photographed.*

44 DICKENS AND MASTER HUMPHREY'S CLOCK: a picture by 'Phiz' for the prospectus announcing the publication of *Master Humphrey's Clock* in serial form, in 1840. *Specially photographed.*

45 WALTER SAVAGE LANDOR (1775–1864), the poet and essayist, was one of Dickens's greatest admirers. It was while visiting him at Bath in 1840 that Dickens invented the character of 'Little Nell' for *The Old Curiosity Shop. Radio Times Hulton Picture Library.*

46 LITTLE NELL and the Old Man looking back at London, from *The Old Curiosity Shop*, 1840. *Specially photographed.*

47 WASHINGTON IRVING (1783–1859), the American writer and diplomat. It was largely as a result of his suggestion that Dickens decided to visit the United States. Both writers had great admiration for each other's work. *Radio Times Hulton Picture Library.*

48 THE BRITANNIA was the first Cunard steamer to begin the transatlantic mail service and one of the earliest passenger steamships. From an old print, after a painting by Clarkson Stanfield, RA. *Specially photographed.*

49 CHARLES DICKENS on board the *Britannia* on his way to America. This sketch was made on deck by a fellow-passenger. *The Dickens Fellowship.*

50 A SLAVE-AUCTION IN SOUTH CAROLINA. Dickens was a passionate opposer of slavery. What he saw of slavery during his trip through the southern states inspired some of the bitterest passages of his *American Notes. Radio Times Hulton Picture Library.*

51 A VIEW OF NEW YORK at the time of Dickens's visit. *The Dickens Fellowship.*

52 TREMONT HOUSE, the hotel in Boston where Dickens and his wife spent their first days in America and were almost overwhelmed by the enthusiastic welcome they received from the town's inhabitants. *The Dickens Fellowship.*

53 DOUGLAS JERROLD (1803–57) was another of Dickens's literary and journalistic friends. He wrote comedies and was a regular contributor to *Punch*. *The Dickens Fellowship.*

54 WILLIAM CHARLES MACREADY (1793–1873), one of the greatest of nineteenth-century English actors, was one of Dickens's closest friends and a consistent admirer of his books. *The Dickens Fellowship.*

WILLIAM MAKEPEACE THACKERAY (1811–1863) first met Dickens in 1836 when he offered to illustrate Pickwick for him. As author of *Vanity Fair* and *Henry Esmond* he was regarded by many as a writer second only to Dickens. *Radio Times Hulton Picture Library.*

55 *A Christmas Carol*: a scene from a stage version produced in London only a few months after the book's first appearance. Dickens suffered greatly in his career from 'pirating' and unauthorised dramatisations of his works. *Mander and Mitchenson Theatre Collection.*

56 GENOA IN 1844: the Strada Balbo in the old quarter of the town where the perpetual chiming of bells inspired Dickens to write *The Chimes. From a lithograph by Deroy. Specially photographed.*

57 THE TERRACE OF THE PALAZZO PESCHIERE in Genoa, where Dickens lived for several months. From F. G. Kitton's *Charles Dickens by Pen and Pencil*, 1890. *Specially photographed.*

58 DICKENS READING *The Chimes* to his friends in London at John Forster's house in Lincoln's Inn Fields in December 1844. His audience includes Forster, Jerrold, Carlyle and Maclise. From a sketch by Maclise. *The Dickens Fellowship.*

59 THE ROMAN CARNIVAL in the Corso during Dickens's visit to the city in February 1845. *Gabinetto Fotografico Nazionale, Rome.*

60 A VIEW OF FLORENCE with the river Arno. From Jules Janin's *Voyage en Italie*, Paris 1839. *Specially photographed.*

61 THE PLAY-BILL for the amateur performance of Ben Jonson's *Every Man in his Humour* in which Dickens and Forster performed in September 1845, with sketches of them in costume by Maclise. *The Forster Collection. By courtesy of the Victoria and Albert Museum, London.*

62 THIS CARTOON satirising Dickens's debut as a newspaper proprietor appeared in *Mephystopheles*, a comic London journal, only three days after the first issue of the *Daily News*, in January 1846. *Specially photographed.*

63 AN EARLY PHOTOGRAPH of the *Daily News* offices in Fleet Street before demolition. *Gernsheim Collection.*

64 A VIEW OF LAUSANNE where Dickens lived for six months in 1846. From Emile Bégin, *Voyage Pittoresque en Suisse*, 1851. *Specially photographed.*

65 DANIEL MACLISE, RA (1806–70), painted and sketched many portraits of Dickens, his family and friends. He was a precocious and talented artist, and became a member of the Royal Academy in 1840. *The Dickens Fellowship.*

66 VICTOR HUGO (1802–85), poet, novelist and leader of the French Romantic move-

ment, who shared Dickens's passionate humanitarian and radical views. They met in Paris during the spring of 1847. *Radio Times Hulton Picture Library.*

67 PARIS HIGH SOCIETY in the 1840s. Dickens's fame as a writer gave him the entrée into French society and the literary world in Paris. From Jules Janin, *Un hiver à Paris*, 1843. *Specially photographed.*

68 DICKENS ON HOLIDAY WITH HIS FRIENDS, from a sketch attributed to Thackeray. There was nothing Dickens liked better than to escape from his work into the country from time to time, surrounded by a few boon-companions. *The Dickens Fellowship.*

69 *Reynold's Miscellany*, a literary magazine, honoured Dickens, Ainsworth and Bulwer-Lytton by portraying them on the cover of one of its issues for 1847. They were then the three most popular writers in the country. *The Dickens Fellowship.*

70 *The Haunted Man*, another of Dickens's *Christmas Stories* which was published in 1848. Dickens enlisted the finest illustrators of the day such as Tenniel the Elder, and John Leech, to illustrate these stories. *Specially photographed.*

71 THE FIRST PAGE of the first issue of *Household Words*, March 1850. *Specially photographed.*

72–73 INDUSTRIAL ENGLAND in the mid-nineteenth-century. 'Such a mass of dirt, gloom and misery as I never before witnessed', wrote Dickens after a visit to the Midlands. *Radio Times Hulton Picture Library.*

73 A DAGUERROTYPE PORTRAIT of Dickens taken in 1849, by Mayall, one of the most talented and fashionable photographers in London. *The Dickens Fellowship.*

74 WILLIAM WILKIE COLLINS (1824–89) was one of Dickens's most intimate friends in his later life. He was the author of *The Woman in White* and *The Moonstone*, a classic 'detective story'. *Radio Times Hulton Picture Library.*

75 STEERFORTH AND MR MELL. One of the many delightful illustrations by 'Phiz' for *David Copperfield*. *Specially photographed.*

76 'If you please, aunt, I am your nephew. "Oh, Lord!" said my aunt. And sat down in the garden path.' David Copperfield's meeting with his aunt. *Specially photographed.*

77 'My magnificent order at the public house.' This episode from *David Copperfield* is based directly upon one of Dickens's own experiences at the time he was working at the blacking warehouse. *Specially photographed.*

78 THE DAVID COPPERFIELD POLKA. The book had a tremendous success and is still the most popular of Dickens's works. Shortly after its publication it even inspired song writers and composers, as in this case. *Mander and Mitchenson Theatre Collection.*

79 *Not so Bad as We Seem* was a comedy written by Bulwer-Lytton. The Duke of Devonshire lent his London house in Piccadilly to Dickens and his amateur company who gave a highly successful performance of the play before Queen Victoria and Prince Albert on May 16, 1851. *The Dickens Fellowship.*

80 TAVISTOCK HOUSE, where Dickens lived from 1851 to 1858. Long since demolished it was one of several large mansions in an old square in Bloomsbury. *Radio Times Hulton Picture Library.*

81 THE AUTHORS COPYRIGHT MEETING. In the mid-nineteenth century many British authors suffered greatly from inadequate copyright protection which often resulted

in their works being 'pirated', notably in America. In 1843 Dickens had presided over a meeting to establish a society of authors which later became an association of authors, publishers and printers. From a contemporary cartoon, in which Dickens can be seen with many of his famous fellow-authors. *The Dickens Fellowship.*

82 BLEAK HOUSE, on a cliff overlooking Broadstairs. The building is still standing today and is often visited by Dickens lovers. From an early photograph showing Broad-tairs almost unchanged since Dickens's life-time. *Radio Times Hulton Picture Library.*

83 AN ILLUSTRATION BY 'PHIZ' from *Bleak House. Specially photographed.*

84 THIS PLAYBILL was printed for Dickens at Tavistock House where he had fitted up a small theatre for his amateur performances, with the enthusiastic co-operation of such friends as Wilkie Collins, and Clarkson Stanfield, the painter, who designed the sets. *Specially photographed.*

85 *The Frozen Deep*. A scene from the lurid melodrama by Wilkie Collins that was performed at Tavistock House. *Mander and Mitchenson Theatre Collection.*

86 MARIA BEADNELL had been Dickens's first great love. Many years later, then Mrs Winter, she wrote to Dickens again who enthusiastically suggested a meeting, which took place in February 1855. Disenchanted by the change in her appearance and manner, Dickens was to caricature her mercilessly in *Little Dorrit. The Dickens Fellowship.*

87 PARIS: the Boulevard des Italiens at night. During his stay in Paris in the winter of 1855–56, Dickens was dazzled by the opulence of the French Second Empire and the gaiety of the Paris boulevards. From Jules Janin, *Un hiver à Paris*, 1843. *Specially photographed.*

88 NEWGATE GAOL. This grim prison is notably featured in *Oliver Twist* and *Barnaby Rudge.* Dickens was a passionate advocate of prison reform and campaigned for the abolition of capital punishment. *Guildhall Library, London.*

89 THE MARSHALSEA was another prison that haunted Dickens's mind. He drew on his childhood memories of it while writing *Little Dorrit*, from which this illustration is taken. *Specially photographed.*

90 ELLEN TERNAN (centre) with her two sisters, Maria and Frances. From a daguerro-type taken at about the time of Ellen's meeting with Dickens. *The Enthoven Col-lection. By courtesy of the Victoria and Albert Museum, London.*

91 DICKENS MAKING A SPEECH at the Adelphi Theatre, in aid of the Royal Dramatic College, Dulwich, in 1856. Dickens was a fine public speaker and in his later life made many speeches on behalf of charity. *The Dickens Fellowship.*

92 DICKENS WITH HIS FAMILY and friends in a friend's garden in 1857. This was one of the last occasions on which Dickens was seen in company with his wife; they were soon to be separated, after 22 years of marriage. *Radio Times Hulton Picture Library.*

Notes

93 OLD DRURY LANE, the very heart of Dickens's London. From an old print. *Guildhall Library, London.*

94 CATHERINE DICKENS. This photograph was taken shortly before 1858. Although she was only forty-three years old at the time of her break with Dickens she had become very stout and entirely lost her earlier good looks. *Gernsheim Collection.*

95 A THIEVES' KITCHEN near Gray's Inn Road, London. This was the seamy side of London life that Dickens dealt with so powerfully in his later novels. From Henry Mayhew's *London Labour and the London Poor*, 1851. *Specially photographed.*

96 HABLÔT K. BROWNE (1815–82) was undoubtedly Dickens's greatest illustrator. He managed to convey the very essence of Dickens's stories in his engravings for them. *The Dickens Fellowship.*

97 EDMUND YATES, the journalist whom Dickens championed in the quarrel with Thackeray at the Garrick Club. *Radio Times Hulton Picture Library.*

98 DICKENS AND THACKERAY. A contemporary caricature of the two great writers at the time of the quarrel which destroyed their friendship. *The Dickens Fellowship.*

99 ELLEN TERNAN. From a daguerrotype taken c. 1857. *The Enthoven Collection. By courtesy of the Victoria and Albert Museum, London.*

100 DICKENS WRITING at his desk at Gad's Hill Place, his last home. From an early photograph. *Gernsheim Collection.*

101 THE COMMITTEE OF CONCOCTION. Every winter Dickens would invite his friends to collaborate with him for the special Christmas features for *Household Words*. This cartoon which appeared in *The Queen*, December 21, 1861, is a humorous reconstruction of one of Dickens's editorial meetings. *Specially photographed.*

102 A 'PHIZ' ILLUSTRATION from *A Tale of Two Cities*, 1859. *Specially photographed.*

103 DICKENS READING to his daughters Mary ('Mamie') and Kate at Gad's Hill. Both daughters were devoted to him and stayed at Gad's Hill after the break-up of Dickens's marriage. *The Dickens Fellowship.*

104 MRS FRANCES ELEANOR TERNAN, Ellen's mother, as she appeared on the stage. She was a talented actress and Dickens probably first saw her when she was playing in London. *Mander and Mitchenson Theatre Collection.*

105 DICKENS'S CHALET AT GAD'S HILL. This Swiss chalet was a present to him from a Swiss actor friend, Charles Fechter. It was posted to Dickens in separate parts in fifty-eight boxes, in 1865. It was in this chalet that Dickens wrote his last lines, for the unfinished *Edwin Drood*. *The Dickens Fellowship.*

DICKENS WITH HIS DAUGHTERS, his sister-in-law and various friends outside Gad's Hill Place. *The Dickens Fellowship.*

106 GEORGINA HOGARTH (1827–1917), Dickens's devoted sister-in-law who stayed at Gad's Hill Place and kept house for him until his death. *The Dickens Fellowship.*

107 FROM WHOM WE HAVE GREAT EXPECTATIONS. This curious caricature appeared in many London shop-windows in 1861 when *Great Expectations* was appearing in serial form. Dickens was greatly amused by it, declaring that it was 'much more like me than the grave portrait done in earnest'. *Specially photographed.*

108 A PHOTOGRAPH OF DICKENS at the desk for his public 'readings'. *The Dickens Fellowship.*

109 ARTHUR SMITH, who was Dickens's manager for the public readings until his death in October 1861. 'It is as if my right arm were gone', said Dickens after hearing the news. *The Dickens Fellowship.*

110 JOHN LEECH (1817–64), the great *Punch* cartoonist, was one of many of Dickens's old friends who died during his last years. *The Dickens Fellowship.*

111 FLEET STREET AND LUDGATE CIRCUS, London, in the 1860s. This was the time of great prosperity and speculation in the City, the background to *Our Mutual Friend.* From Gustave Doré's *London,* 1872. An advertisement for *The Daily News* can be seen on the bridge. *Specially photographed.*

112 THE STAPLEHURST RAILWAY DISASTER, 1865. An imaginary reconstruction of the scene from a newspaper of the time, showing Dickens helping the injured. *The Dickens Fellowship.*

113 THE LONDON DUST-HEAPS, which played a prominent part in the plot of *Our Mutual Friend.* From *Cassell's Old and New London. Specially photographed.*

114 A BANQUET IN DICKENS'S HONOUR. An example of the lavish social occasions in honour of Dickens that he attended in his last years. *The Dickens Fellowship.*

115 FAREWELL TO DICKENS, a cartoon which appeared in a London paper on the occasion of Dickens's voyage to America. John Bull is seen shaking hands with Dickens, while various characters from his novels are looking on. *Specially photographed.*

116 THE BRITISH LION IN AMERICA. A caricature of Dickens from *The Daily Joker,* a New York humorous paper. *Specially photographed.*

117 AN AMERICAN CARTOON on Dickens's readings. Although dressed as the different characters he is portraying, he always shows the 'same prolific head'. *Specially photographed.*

118 THE GREAT PRESS BANQUET given in Dickens's honour at Delmonico's in New York, April 18, 1868. From a sketch made by a reporter from the *Chicago Illustrated News. The Dickens Fellowship.*

119 AN EARLY PHOTOGRAPH of Broadway, New York. *Gernsheim Collection.*

120 CHARLES DICKENS in 1868. This famous photograph by the American photographer Ben Gurney shows how aged Dickens had become in his appearance. *The Dickens Fellowship.*

121 CHARLES FECHTER, the actor. He and Dickens became very friendly. He appeared at the New Royal Adelphi Theatre in London in December 1867 in a play that Dickens and Wilkie Collins had written specially for him. It was a great success and ran for well over a hundred nights. *Mander and Mitchenson Theatre Collection.*

122 *The Mystery of Edwin Drood.* The manuscript of the last page that Dickens ever wrote, on June 8, 1870. That same evening he collapsed, and died within twenty-four hours. *The Forster Collection. By courtesy of the Victoria and Albert Museum.*

123 A FRENCH CARICATURE of Dickens, by André Gill, from *L'Eclipse,* Paris, June 14, 1868. *Specially photographed.*

124 THE FIRST WRAPPER of the first instalment of *The Mystery of Edwin Drood.* Only six serial issues were published. *Specially photographed.*

Notes

125 AN IMPRESSION of Dickens's last public reading, at St James's Hall, London, in March 1870. *The Dickens Fellowship.*

127 WESTMINSTER ABBEY. Poets' Corner a few days after Dickens's burial, thronged with people who had come to pay their last respects. From the *Illustrated London News. Mander and Mitchenson Theatre Collection.*

128 THE EMPTY CHAIR. Luke Fildes's famous picture of Dickens's study in Gad's Hill Place, painted on the day of Dickens's death, inspired many cartoons, such as this one which was published in a London paper a fortnight after Dickens's death. *Specially photographed.*